Jaspers and Bultmann: A dialogue

Eugene Thomas Long

Jaspers and Bultmann: A dialogue between philosophy and theology in the existentialist tradition

Duke University Press, Durham, North Carolina   1968

Preface

The purpose of this book is to make a contribution toward an understanding of some of the issues raised in the contemporary dialogue between philosophy and theology. I have concentrated in particular on the dialogue between Karl Jaspers, a philosopher, and Rudolf Bultmann, a theologian. There are several reasons for this choice. First, both of these German scholars are widely recognized for their original contributions to their fields of inquiry. Second, while Jaspers and Bultmann do not always agree, their thought is rooted in a common existentialist tradition, and they do share many points of view. Finally, they have initiated this dialogue between themselves. Jaspers was requested to address a congress of Swiss theologians at Basel, and he chose to speak to some of the issues raised by Bultmann's project of demythologizing. This lecture was published in 1953. There followed a reply by Bultmann and a counterreply by Jaspers. Many significant issues were raised in this discussion and yet the dialogue was not always successful. At times Jaspers and Bultmann seem to be misunderstanding each other. At other times issues are raised but are discussed in no detail. Because of this it is a part of my task to select what I consider to be some of the more important questions raised in this discussion and to develop them more fully in the context of their work as a whole.

Each chapter of this study is divided into a number of sections. Apart from the first section of the Introduction, which introduces the thought of the lesser known Jaspers, each section is organized to develop Jaspers' and then Bultmann's point of view on the topic being discussed. A concluding section is provided in each chapter in which the primary issues between Jaspers and Bultmann are discussed and evaluated.

The extent of my indebtedness will be obvious to those who read this volume. However, it is my privilege to acknowledge in particular my indebtedness to Professor Ronald Gregor Smith of Glasgow University and Professor John Macquarrie of Union Theological Seminary, New York. Their advice and encouragement in the earlier stages of this study when it was submitted as a doctoral dissertation to Glasgow University and their continuing interest in its development have been invaluable. I wish also to express my appreciation to the readers for the Duke University Press for their valuable critiques, to Professor H. Burnell Pannill of Randolph-Macon College, who has never failed to lend assistance, and to Randolph-Macon College for its aid in the publication of this volume. Finally I wish to express my incalculable indebtedness to my wife whose encouragement and understanding have never waned. It is to her and to our son that this volume is dedicated.

E.T.L.

Ashland, Virginia
June, 1967

Contents

To Carolyn Macleod and Scott Alexander

I Introduction

Philosophy and the Illumination of Existence

At the end of a course of lectures in metaphysics in 1928, Karl Jaspers was approached by a young Roman Catholic priest who had been a student in the course. The priest expressed his appreciation for the lectures but observed that most of what Jaspers had discussed was, from the Roman Catholic point of view, theology.[1] Jaspers admits that he was startled at this suggestion. He was philosophizing. Yet he was doing as a non-theologian what others considered to be theology. This raised the question of the distinctiveness and the relationship between philosophy and theology.

The result of Jaspers' attempt to clarify this relationship between philosophy and theology is found in his idea of philosophical faith. Since the publication of his *Philosophie* in 1931 he has advocated philosophical faith as the meaning of philosophical doctrine, and through it he has sought to communicate with those who no longer find ecclesiastical faith illuminating. Philosophy thus becomes more than "just another science." For while the philosopher does not present himself as a prophet, he does seek to remind, to appeal, and thus to provide the occasion for the other person's grasping the meaning of philosophical doctrine and awakening to his authentic existence.

Jaspers' philosophy is neither metaphysical in the traditional sense nor antimetaphysical in the contemporary sense. He philosophizes about Being. Yet Being is said to be appropriated only

1. Jaspers, "Philosophical Autobiography," in *The Philosophy of Karl Jaspers*, ed. Paul A. Schilpp (New York: Tudor, 1957; now published by Open Court, La Salle, Ill.), p. 77.

through the indirect communication of the philosophical task as a whole. Being does not disclose itself in either the subject or the object of human existence, but in that indefinable sphere which encompasses both. For this reason his philosophy may be described as a philosophy of the Encompassing. It is the receptive and non-objective clarification of the whole of Being in all of its relations and not the objective clarification of Being as essentially finished and stable. Ontology is replaced by "periechontology," which does not concern itself with Being as a determinate object to be clarified in objective thought but illuminates the sphere in which Being becomes present for us.[2] To Being, understood in this manner, Jaspers has given the name, the Encompassing (*das Umgreifende*). It is that which encompasses the subject-object dichotomy and is found in neither subject nor object.

> The fundamental philosophical operation at all times is, more or less consciously, to transcend towards that out of which the objective as well as the thinking of the subject intending the objective arises. What is neither object nor act of thinking (subject), but contains both within itself, I have called the Encompassing. This latter does not speak for itself either through the object or through the subject, but through both in one as that which is the Transcendence at one and the same time of consciousness as well as of Being.[3]

Philosophy had its beginning in the question, "What is? What is it that lies at the base of everything and from which everything issues?" Jaspers is also concerned with this question. However he wishes to avoid the apprehension of Being as an object and the claim to exclusiveness which follows it. Jaspers' answer to this question is, according to Gerhard Knauss, imbedded in the Kantian and Platonic views of the Idea but has undergone the criticism of

2. Jaspers, *Von der Wahrheit* (Munich: R. Piper Verlag, 1958), pp. 158 ff. Cited hereinafter as *Wahrheit*.
3. Jaspers, "Philosophical Autobiography," p. 73.

Kierkegaard in being related to the subject, that is, to individual human existence.[4]

According to Jaspers, man seeks the foundation of all that is and finds himself bound to the subject-object dichotomy. But, in this dichotomy he realizes that the foundation of all that is, Being as a whole, can never be confined to one side of it. Being is that which is bound to neither subject nor object but is manifested in the dichotomy itself. Thus the Encompassing has no definite and objective content; it never appears as an object in finite knowledge.[5]

Jaspers' philosophy then stands in opposition to the tendency to absolutize either subject or object. The absolutizing of the object can take a number of forms but each errs for the same basic reason. The so-called realist, who rightly points out the empirically real, is mistaken when he assumes empirical reality to be conclusively known, and when he claims to determine absolutely the issue of truth. The moralist errs when laws, formulated on the basis of a definite content, are thought to be absolutely valid in every situation. The aestheticist fails when he turns against the endless movement of relations in favor of Being as a substance to be possessed. The ontologist fails in coming to rest upon the completeness of conceptualized Being.

It is when the objective becomes absolutized in this manner that a revolt or breakthrough to subjectivity occurs (Kierkegaard's revolt against Hegel, for instance). Subjectivity, according to Jaspers, has its place in its polemic against the various forms of bondage to the objective. But, subjectivity may also fail when it loses all relationship to the objective and absolutizes itself.[6]

---

4. Gerhard Knauss, "The Concept of the Encompassing in Jaspers' Philosophy," in *The Philosophy of Karl Jaspers*, pp. 141 ff.

5. Jaspers, *Reason and Existenz*, trans. William Earle (New York: Noonday Press, 1955, and London: Routledge and Kegan Paul, 1956), p. 52. Cited hereinafter as *Reason*.

6. Jaspers, *Truth and Symbol from Von der Wahrheit*, trans. J. T. Wilde, W. Kluback and W. Kimmel (New York: Twayne, 1959), pp. 25 ff. Cited hereinafter as *Truth*.

In contrast to the tendency to absolutize either the subject or the object, the Encompassing is said to be neither subject nor object. It is present through both as that inexhaustible depth which transcends them. Nevertheless, it does not remain unknown to us but discloses itself as we stand within the subject-object dichotomy in which all finite knowledge is immersed. There is an inexhaustible depth in all experience that directs us beyond the limits of ordinary knowledge. This is Being or the Encompassing which "appears and disappears for us in two opposed perspectives: either as Being itself, in and through which we are—or else as the Encompassing which we ourselves are, and in which every mode of Being appears to us."[7]

It follows that there are two conceivable approaches to Being as the Encompassing, either toward Being itself, conceived as nature, world, or God, or toward the Encompassing-that-we-are, in which every mode of Being appears to us. Jaspers maintains that since Kant the latter approach is the necessary one. By approaching Being through the Encompassing-that-we-are, he means to work through the various modes of the subject-object dichotomy in which we are immersed, coming in each mode upon the horizon which forces us to acknowledge the limits that prevent us from grasping the totality of Being. This horizon, by its very existence, indicates something further, something that we cannot grasp within one particular mode of the subject-object dichotomy or even in a combination of them.

The Encompassing-that-we-are (*Das Umgreifende-das-wir-sind*) appears in three different modes: empirical existence (*Dasein*), consciousness-as-such (*Bewusstsein überhaupt*), and spirit (*Geist*).[8] Empirical existence in ordinary speech refers to that which appears as a definite something in space and time, that which encounters

7. *Reason*, p. 52.
8. The following exposition of the modes of the Encompassing-that-we-are follows Jaspers' development in *Wahrheit*, pp. 53 ff., and *Reason*, pp. 51 ff. The idea of truth in relation to these modes of the Encompassing-that-we-are is discussed in *Wahrheit*, pp. 605 ff.

us corporeally in the world, those determinate objects which dominate us. But empirical existence as the Encompassing-that-we-are has another sense. It is the individual encountering of the self which we express in saying "I am here" or "We are here." It is the consciousness of reality which mental patients may lose temporarily. It is the environment in which all that is appears to me. "Empirical existence means the actual taken comprehensively, which immediately shows itself to empirical consciousness in the particularities of matter, living body, and soul, but which, as such particularities, is no longer the Encompassing of empirical existence."[9] Although I am unable to comprehend empirical existence as an Encompassing but only particular forms of it, I always stand in its presence. Consequently, it is only as I break away from all attempts to objectify myself that I am really human.

The second mode of the Encompassing-that-we-are is consciousness-as-such. In contrast to empirical existence which refers to our inward and undifferentiated experience, consciousness-as-such refers to the dimension of consciousness in which we have universally valid knowledge of tangible objects. Here we leap, so to speak, from the multiplicity of particular realities in existence and participate in universally valid truth. Thus, while it is not without empirical existence, consciousness-as-such develops independently of it. That is, it does not require in its thinking the motives or influences of existence. Here I am essentially one with others participating in impersonal and universally valid truth whereas truth for empirical existence is relative to the individual, what is suitable to its preservation and development, what is adequate to its subjectivity.

Spirit designates the third mode of the Encompassing-that-we-are. It is "the totality of intelligible thought, action, and feeling—a totality which is not a closed object for knowledge but remains Idea."[10] Here the self is related to the world of theoretical forms. What is only fragmented in consciousness-as-such is held together

9. *Reason*, p. 54.   10. *Ibid.*, p. 57.

in the ideas. Spirit, in contrast to consciousness-as-such, is a temporal process more akin to empirical existence. Yet, in contrast to empirical existence, "it moves by a reflexivity of knowledge instead of by some biologico-psychological process."[11] Insofar as Spirit is bound up with personal existence, its truth is not universally valid for consciousness-as-such but depends upon the participation of the person. However, truth is not relative for it in the sense that it is for empirical existence. It is of the totality, but the totality remains in movement and is never grasped as a knowable object. What is thought or willed or felt is not true in itself but only insofar as it is a moment in the totality.

These three modes of the Encompassing-that-we-are are not inseparable facts but represent three starting points from which we may approach Being. In these three modes, man is understood as a being in the world. But in following through any of these modes, in covering the whole range of immediate experience, man becomes aware of his transcendence, of that inexhaustible depth, which cannot be contained within the limits of any one of these modes or in a combination of them. At these limits he is referred beyond in knowing that his being is not exhausted here. Life is understood to have its source in that which lies beyond the reach of man's limitedness in any of the modes of the Encompassing-that-we-are. This is shown in man's dissatisfaction with himself, in the recognition of his inadequacy, in his subordination to the Absolute, and in the unceasing urge for unity which is Being and Eternity. It is also indicated, according to Jaspers, in man's consciousness of immortality and in his consciousness of an "indefinable *memory*, as though he shared in the knowledge of creation (Schelling), or as though he remembered something beheld before any world existed (Plato)."[12]

In the recognition of his incompleteness man is said to encounter

---

11. *Ibid.*, p. 58.
12. Jaspers, *The Perennial Scope of Philosophy*, trans. R. Manheim (New York: Philosophical Library, 1949, and London: Routledge and Kegan Paul, 1949), p. 15. Cited hereinafter as *Perennial Scope*.

his potential Existenz, his being which has its source not in empirical existence, consciousness-as-such, or spirit, but in the primal source which lies beyond all of this.[13] It is in this hidden ground of Existenz that Being is made manifest as Transcendence, not simply as a void to be treated with indifference but as that through which I am genuinely myself. When compared with any of the three modes of the Encompassing-that-we-are. Existenz shows that without it all would be empty, without ground, mere possibility or empirical existence. Existenz is the Encompassing-that-we-are as Transcendence. It is the source from which all other modes of the Encompassing-that-we-are receive animation and from which they speak.

Man, then, in all modes of the Encompassing-that-we-are, is capable of breaking through the objectivity of the subject-object dichotomy, and the non-objective presence of Being is touched upon. Empirical existence breaks through the objectivity of its environment in not finding fulfilment of its will. Consciousness-as-such penetrates its objectivity in grasping its universal truths as a series capable of being infinitely gathered. Spirit breaks through the objectivity of the idea in being unable to take into itself the reality of the less than total, the contingent, and merely factual.

However, it is in Existenz that Being is present as Transcendence, as that through which I am genuinely myself. And this occurs as Existenz breaks through its objectivity, which is the tangible presence of Transcendence in myth. While no one of these dimensions of human experience is separated from the other and while all modes of the Encompassing-that-we-are make up man, it is nevertheless in Existenz that Transcendence is "known" to me in such a way that I am aware of a real relation. This relationship is

13. *Existenz* is left untranslated to distinguish it from *Dasein* which is translated existence or empirical existence, and from existence as it is more generally used to refer to existence which is not oriented toward Transcendence. In places where Existenz is translated its meaning is either obvious or qualified by the word "authentic." Jaspers indicates his indebtedness to Kierkegaard for the mature expression of Existenz. See Jaspers, *Philosophie* (Berlin: Springer-Verlag, 1948), p. 13, n. 1.

mediated by the cipher, an intuitive (*schaubar*) symbol whose meaning is never objectified or made final.

Existenz, which man never possesses once and for all, can be given no limiting definition. The term itself is a cipher, an index to the being of man that cannot be conceptualized. Existenz refers to that aspect of man's selfhood that cannot be grasped in empirical investigation, in abstract understanding, or in any attempt to form a unity out of the totality of finite knowledge. Thus Jaspers speaks at times of potential Existenz, a way of being that confronts us as a potentiality without ever being possessed by us.

Existenz is not something to be grasped within the limits of finite explanation but presupposes the leap to Transcendence in which one does not prove but experiences one's freedom from the limits of immanence. Existenz is actually an occurrence in the life of each individual which takes place only as he stands in relation to Transcendence. At the same time it is in Existenz that Transcendence, as the power through which one is authentic, is other than a void and has a real relation to man's being. Thus, Jaspers speaks of Existenz as "the dark ground of selfhood, the concealment out of which I come to encounter myself and for which Transcendence first becomes real."[14] Existenz, Transcendence, and freedom then are interrelated terms, none of which can be conceptualized. Existenz is grounded in Transcendence and Transcendence first becomes real to Existenz. And the life which is realized in this relation is one of freedom.

Transcendence or the Encompassing of all Encompassing is referred to in many ways by Jaspers. As the "object" of philosophical thinking, it is called Being. It is Reality insofar as it is perceptible to us as a concern, as it attracts us and sets limits upon us. To the extent that it makes demands upon us, masters us, it is Deity, and to the extent that we as individuals know of a personal encounter with it, it is God. But in all cases these are only images which in themselves say nothing about Transcendence and must lose their

14. *Reason*, p. 64.

objectivity in communication. Transcendence discloses itself only at the limits of the finite and remains a void apart from the leap of Existenz.

Freedom, like Existenz and Transcendence, is not a concept nor is it capable of being proved. It is that which one realizes only in creative activity when one chooses oneself from beyond the limits of empirical or theoretical certainty. It is a choosing and being responsible for choosing one's way of being. This act however is not independent of the historical situation in which one is immersed; it is an action in time. It is bound up with Transcendence in that I confront my freedom as a gift from beyond myself. Yet it is not grasped in a mystical flight from the world. It is in the midst of my situation in the world that I decide for that selfhood which is not limited by the world and yet is open to it.[15]

Freedom and Existenz then are not directly known but are encountered in the act of existing. Yet neither is real apart from Transcendence, which is disclosed to me as I leap from the dimension of immanence to that of freedom and Existenz. This leap is affirmed in philosophical faith, faith which is never sure of itself and is always striving to elucidate itself. Faith in this sense is "faith in the way of truth, on which all can meet each other who search sincerely."[16]

Philosophical faith is for Jaspers more than a disengaged attitude toward life. Jaspers is actually proposing it as a means of illuminating the unconditional basis of life to those who no longer find the claims of orthodoxy tenable and who are unwilling to take up the position of nihilism. Thus, while philosophical faith cannot replace the religious faith of a worshiping community, it is in some sense an option for it. At least it may be understood as a "liberal" or secular interpretation of traditional Christian faith. For this reason Erich Frank, reviewing Jaspers' *Philosophie,* can say that in the midst of a time when it is claimed that the disappearance of Christianity has left a vacuum, the philosophy of Jaspers is a de-

15. *Philosophie*, pp. 445–466.   16. "Philosophical Autobiography," p. 81.

cisive step which captures the Protestant conviction secularized in a manner reminiscent of Kant.[17]

Philosophical faith, as Jaspers understands it, can neither be identified with nor separated from what he calls religious faith. Rather, "religion remains for philosophy always a polar other, with which it is concerned, from which it receives stimuli, and to which it in turn returns stimuli."[18] Consequently, philosophical faith must always seek to communicate with religious faith.

A unique opportunity for this communication between philosophical and religious faith was provided when Jaspers was invited to address a congress of Swiss theologians at Basel. He chose to speak directly of the problems of religious thought as they presented themselves to him in Rudolf Bultmann's program of demythologizing. However, Jaspers' address by no means limits itself to demythologizing as a hermeneutical method. It might be better understood as an encounter between philosophical faith and what Jaspers calls Bultmann's orthodox faith. In this address and in the replies by Bultmann and Jaspers we have a direct confrontation of philosophical and Christian faith. It is the purpose of our study to make a detailed analysis of some of the issues which emerge in this meeting of Jaspers and Bultmann.[19]

17. Erich Frank, "Die Philosophie von Jaspers," *Wissen, Wollen, Glauben* (Zurich: Artemis-Verlag, 1955), pp. 287–288. Erich Dinkler makes a similar comment: "Jaspers must be characterized as an extreme liberal Protestant who, concerned with Jesus as a type for failing mankind, uses him to support his 'philosophical faith,'" Dinkler, "Martin Heidegger," in *Christianity and the Existentialists*, ed. Carl Michalson (New York: Scribner's, 1956), p. 115.
18. Jaspers, "Reply to My Critics," in *The Philosophy of Karl Jaspers*, p. 779.
19. John Macquarrie has contributed a chapter toward this end in *The Scope of Demythologizing* (London: S.C.M. Press, 1960, and New York: Harper and Row, 1961), pp. 154–185, and Wenzel Lohff has made an analysis of Jaspers' critique of religion in *Glaube und Freiheit* (Gutersloh: Carl Bertrelsmann Verlag, 1957).

Preliminary View of the Nature of Faith

Jaspers' philosophy seeks to communicate indirectly the truth that cannot be grasped in objective and universally valid statements. The result is a philosophy which purposely evades precise definition and avoids anything like a system of doctrines. Jaspers assures us of this with regard to philosophical faith when he says that it is expressed "only in an ultimately indirect communication of the total philosophical work."[20] Inevitably, then, any attempt to characterize philosophical faith runs the risk of falsely objectifying Jaspers' point of view. Nevertheless, Jaspers does not deny the organization which is essential to all reasoning, and the reader has a right to expect that since philosophical faith affirms one point of view and rejects another, it may be presented in a manner that permits comparison and analysis.

It follows from what has already been said that philosophical faith is not belief in a body of doctrine which is taken to be universally valid. Philosophical faith can never become a credo and can be characterized only negatively. Jaspers does refer to several propositions of philosophical faith: God is; there is an unconditional imperative; man is finite and imperfectable; man can live in God's guidance; and the reality of the world subsists ephemerally between God and existence. However, these propositions do not constitute a creed; they remain always in the realm of non-knowledge. "None of these five principles is demonstrable in the sense of a limited insight into objects in the world. Their truth can only be 'pointed out,' 'elucidated,' by a chain of reasoning, 'recalled to

20. *Reason*, p. 141.

mind.' "[21] These propositions have their truth only in their nega-
tion. "The realm of the objective must remain in motion, must
evaporate as it were, so that as the object vanishes, a fulfilled consciousness of being is made clear by this very vanishing."[22]

Second, philosophical faith is free from the claims of all external
authorities. According to Jaspers, medieval philosophy thought of
itself as a *praeambula fidei*. Descartes was a servant of the Church.
Spinoza believed himself to be in possession of the truth, and
Hegel developed his logic as a form of divine worship. In contrast
to this, Jaspers maintains, philosophical faith is incapable of finding its meaning in external authorities. It seeks Transcendence out
of its own sources. Philosophical faith has what Jaspers calls the
"spirit of philosophy" in his discussion of Lessing's classic, *Nathan
the Wise*.[23] Nathan, according to Jaspers, overcomes the tragic
neither in mystical vision nor in the assurances given in Christian
orthodoxy. No other world is brought in to overcome and subdue
the tragedy of the immanent world. Lessing's world and the place
for dealing with tragedy is the natural world, the place where men
are united not in any final truth but in the free striving for truth.
The philosophical spirit then is the free striving for truth which
characterizes the life of Nathan. It stands on the boundary between
revelation and nihilism, between faith and the denial of the world.
It is a spirit of openness and freedom in which the individual
recognizes his relation to those who inquire in freedom and in
honesty.

This attitude toward all external authorities is further elucidated
by Jaspers in his expressed appreciation for the dialectic in skepticism. Skepticism maintains a negative attitude toward all objective
claims to truth. It destroys all objects, placing no limit on doubt.
Yet in this very process it reveals that it does not doubt all, for
in the act of negating it is at the same time affirming another truth.

21. Jaspers, *Way to Wisdom*, trans. R. Manheim (New Haven: Yale Univ.
Press, 1960, and London: Gollancz, 1951), p. 85. Cited hereinafter as
Wisdom.
22. *Perennial Scope*, p. 18.
23. *Wahrheit*, pp. 949 ff.

In other words it doubts on the basis of a truth which calls all else into doubt. For this reason skepticism is a continuous and ever new movement, in which one stands at the limit where truth is possible. Yet once the skeptic is aware of this and attempts to develop this truth his questioning begins again.[24]

This attitude of philosophical faith, which we have attempted to characterize by speaking of the "spirit of philosophy" and the attitude of skepticism, is summarized by Jaspers when he says, "Philosophical faith venerates traditional philosophy but does not maintain an attitude of obedience to it. It does not look on history as an authority, but as one continuous spiritual struggle."[25] This understanding of faith leads to the understanding of the believer as an exception (*Ausnahme*), one who founders upon objective authority and struggles with it. Seen externally, the exception is the abnormal and irregular life. But seen existentially it is the personal life of a man who breaks through the objective and universal order and leads us beyond the finite world. The life of the exception is, according to Jaspers, a possibility for everyone. Yet he speaks in particular of Nietzsche and Kierkegaard, from whom he has learned of the exception and who are to him exceptions in every sense of the word.

> Those who knew them felt attracted in an enigmatic way by their presence, as though being elevated for a moment to a higher mode of being; but no one really loved them.
>
> In the circumstances of their lives, one finds astonishing and alien features. They have been called simply insane. . . . They cannot be classed under any earlier type (poet, philosopher, prophet, savior, genius). With them, a new form of human reality appears in history. They are, so to speak, representative destinies, sacrifices whose way out of the world leads to experiences for others.[26]

Third, philosophical faith "is the fulfilling and moving element

24. *Ibid.*, pp. 728–732.
25. *Perennial Scope*, p. 22.
26. *Reason*, pp. 37–38; see also *Wahrheit*, pp. 748 ff.

in the depths of man, in which man is linked, above and beyond himself, with the origin of his being."[27] Faith, understood in this manner, is an inner act in which man becomes his authentic self through the recognition of the transcendent source of his being. Even this, however, must not be looked upon as assigning definite content to philosophical faith. Philosophical faith is distinguished from all forms of "outer faith." An outer faith takes certain goals of volition or contents of reason as the purpose of life. It is a temporal faith which is limited to the rational and empirical. Thus, Communism, with its ideal society, might be an example of outer faith. The Christian faith can also be seen in this manner when it seeks to shape the future by the content of dogmas or rationalized goals. These examples of outer faith may claim to be faith only in the sense of transcending the present and looking to the future. Outer faith is, in short, a faith without Transcendence.

In contrast to this, philosophical faith might be understood as an inner faith which is, according to Jaspers, the only faith that can give meaning to the outer faiths of freedom, world order, and so on. Jaspers' rejection of outer faiths is in line with Kierkegaard's criticism of the "system" which had achieved its final polish in German Idealism. Faith in a system of any type refers to that which is closed and complete, whereas the faith of which Jaspers speaks is open and incomplete. Philosophical faith is that movement in man in which he acknowledges his communion with Transcendence beyond the stability of the finite world. This faith is something realized only in the immediate experience of the individual. It "must continually draw upon the primal source within each historical situation."[28] Faith is an existential act in which Transcendence becomes actualized in the individual's awakening to his true self.[29]

27. Jaspers, *The Origin and Goal of History*, trans. Michael Bullock (London: Routledge and Kegan Paul, 1953, and New Haven: Yale Univ. Press, 1953), p. 215. Cited hereinafter as *Origin*.
28. *Perennial Scope*, p. 11.
29. *Origin*, pp. 214 ff.; *Perennial Scope*, pp. 17 ff.

Finally, philosophical faith, which is immersed in the struggle with the objective authorities of the world, can be said to have no finality other than that which exists in the independent thinking of each individual, and even that must always be put into question. Philosophical faith seems to have a form of certainty in a particular historical situation when Jaspers says: "I do not know whether I believe. But faith takes hold of me to such an extent that I dare to live by it."[30] Yet it can never become a possession. "Hence I must recognize not only that I do not know God but even that I do not know whether I believe. Faith is no possession. It confers no secure knowledge, but it gives certainty in the practice of life."[31]

Philosophical faith, according to Jaspers, is other than orthodox Christian faith. Yet, it is apparent that it stands very near to Christian faith as understood by Rudolf Bultmann. Like Jaspers, Bultmann seeks to avoid the more shallow conclusions of some Enlightenment thinkers, and yet, also like Jaspers, he seeks a faith which is other than submission to a body of dogmas or principles which are to be applied in the various situations of life. Faith for Bultmann is a decision made in the moment; it is an act in which man lives authentically out of the future, being freed from bondage to his past. It is not something that man possesses, nor is it a form of purely subjective or mystical awareness. It is a decision made in time, in history.

It is this view of faith which has led Jaspers to take an interest in the theology of Bultmann. However, if he is attracted to Bultmann on the one hand, he is repulsed on the other hand when Bultmann maintains that faith is a reality only as commitment to the event of God's redemptive act in Jesus Christ. Bultmann appears to be saying one thing, says Jaspers, but in the end he says something else. He would seem to be saving faith but finally destroys it. The philosopher, according to Jaspers, cannot help but be repulsed when he finds that the salvaged minimum of faith is justification by faith in the redemptive history. "For a philosopher

30. *Perennial Scope*, p. 37.   31. *Wisdom*, pp. 50–51.

this is the most alienating, the most outlandish of beliefs—this Lutheran dogma with its terrible consequences scarcely seems any longer even denotative existentially."[32]

It has been suggested by a number of persons such as Karl Barth, Fritz Buri, and Schubert Ogden, that this apparent discrepancy which Jaspers observes in Bultmann's view of faith is based on an inner inconsistency in his theology which results from his attempt to reconcile existential self-understanding and the particularity of the Christian faith.[33] Bultmann rejects this criticism on several occasions but in doing so presents us with the problematic task of seeing how these two aspects of faith are reconciled in his thought.

A fairly typical example of Bultmann's definition of faith as self-understanding is found in the Shaffer Lectures where he says, "if we hold that we can speak of all such matters [redemption, etc.] only when we are concerned with our personal existence, then it can be said that faith is a new understanding of personal existence. In other words, God's action bestows upon us a new understanding of ourselves."[34] We learn on several occasions that this new self-understanding is life lived out of the future, an understanding of ourselves based on unseen intangible realities, the abandonment of a life based on self-contrived security.[35]

Some critics, most notably perhaps Helmut Thielicke, have voiced the opinion that this definition of faith as self-understanding makes faith into a subjective act analogous to Schleiermacher's

32. Jaspers and Bultmann, *Myth and Christianity: An Inquiry into the Possibility of Religion without Myth* (New York: Noonday Press, 1958), p. 50. Cited hereinafter as *Myth*. See also *Kerygma and Myth*, ed. H. W. Bartsch and trans. R. H. Fuller (London: S.P.C.K., 1957, and New York: Harper & Row, 1961), pp. 22 ff.

33. Karl Barth, "Rudolf Bultmann—An Attempt to Understand Him," in *Kerygma and Myth*, ed. H. W. Bartsch and trans. R. H. Fuller, II (London: S.P.C.K., 1962), pp. 83–132; Schubert Ogden, *Christ without Myth* (New York: Harper and Row, 1961); Fritz Buri, "Entmythologisierung oder Entkerygmatisierung der Theologie," in *Kerygma und Mythos*, II/2 (Hamburg: Herbert Reich Evangelischer Verlag, 1965), pp. 85–101.

34. Bultmann, *Jesus Christ and Mythology* (New York: Scribner's, 1958), p. 73. Cited hereinafter as *Mythology*.

35. *Kerygma and Myth* (London, 1957), pp. 19 ff.

self-consciousness.[36] This criticism of Bultmann's thought, it seems to me, is of little serious substance. It may be true, probably is, that insofar as Bultmann is dependent on Heidegger's analysis of self-understanding he has over-individualized man's relation to the world of persons and things.[37] Nevertheless, existence for Heidegger and for Bultmann is not confined to subjective consciousness but is authentically or inauthentically related to the world.

Bultmann agrees that the interpretation of faith in a psychologizing sense is inadequate. It ignores the understanding of man as historic being whose experience consists of encounters. It is on this basis that he separates his point of view from Jaspers' conception of philosophical faith and also rejects the criticism by Thielicke.

> As a self who exists historically I am not isolated either from my environment or from my own past and future, which are in a special way a part of my environment. If, for instance, my encounter with another's love should vouchsafe to me a new understanding of self, what happens is by no means restricted to consciousness, at least if consciousness is to be taken as a psychic rather than an existential phenomenon, which is what Thielicke and others wrongly suppose. By understanding myself in this encounter I understand the other in such a way that the whole world appears in a new light, which means that it has in fact become an entirely different world.[38]

Man's new understanding of himself is one which arises only in the encounters which question him and demand his decision.[39] It is here in encounter that Bultmann finds the coincidence of subject and object, and it is by reference to encounter that he seeks to pass beyond the more traditional subject-object scheme of things, represented by Thielicke, which calls for an objective redemptive

36. *Ibid.*, pp. 146–147.
37. See Martin Buber's criticism of Heidegger in *Between Man and Man*, Introduction by Maurice Friedman and trans. Ronald Gregor Smith (New York: Macmillan, 1967), pp. 163 ff.
38. *Kerygma and Myth* (London, 1957), p. 203.
39. Bultmann, "Humanism and Christianity," *Journal of Religion*, XXXII (April, 1952), 82 ff.

event which is external to man in its objective factualness. Bultmann is not denying the act of God outside man, but he is saying that it is something encountered in the proclamation of the Church only as it becomes God's act for me.

The objection that says that faith for Bultmann is nothing but subjective consciousness further maintains that the content of such faith is a timeless truth which remains valid apart from the revelation which gives rise to it.[40] In replying to this part of the criticism, Bultmann maintains that the critic fails to understand the distinction between the self-understanding of personal existence and the philosophical understanding of existence. He agrees that one may apply timeless truths to the philosophical analysis of existence, but it is, he says, precisely this analysis which shows that personal or "existentiell" understanding is realized only here and now as my self-understanding. Philosophical analysis indicates to us what existence in the abstract means and as such may be classified under the heading of timeless truths. Personal or existentiell understanding however "does not say what existence means in the abstract, but points to my life as a concrete person in the here and now. It is an act of understanding in which my very self and the relationships in which I am involved are understood together."[41]

In other words, if faith meant nothing more than what Heidegger means by existential self-understanding, then it would have the character of timeless truth. But in fact faith is a new self-understanding which is never a possession of mine and must be renewed in every moment of concrete encounter. And this existentiell self-understanding of faith for Bultmann is a response to the encounter with God's Word as proclaimed in the kerygma. "This new self-

40. *Kerygma and Myth* (London, 1957), pp. 146–147.
41. *Mythology*, p. 74. See also *Kerygma and Myth* (London, 1957), pp. 202 ff. This distinction between existential (*existenzial*) and existentiell (*existenziell*) understanding is made by Heidegger in *Being and Time*, trans. J. Macquarrie and E. S. Robinson (New York: Harper and Row, 1962, and London: S.C.M. Press, 1962), pp. 32 ff. Existentiell possibility refers to the unique possibility which belongs to my concrete or ontic existence. Existential possibility (ontological) refers to the horizon in which I have my existentiell possibility.

understanding can be maintained only as a continual response to the Word of God which proclaims His action in Jesus Christ."[42] It is in this sense that faith remains indissolubly related to the event of the Christian revelation.

> Faith, in the strict sense of the word, was only there at a certain moment in history. It had to be *revealed*; it *came* (Gal. 3:23, 25). This might of course be taken as part of the story of man's spiritual evolution. But the New Testament means more than that. It claims that faith only became possible at a definite point in history in consequence of an *event*—viz., the event of Christ. Faith in the sense of obedient self-commitment and inward detachment from the world is only possible when it is faith in Jesus Christ.[43]

In Bultmann's mind the believer and the unbeliever are both men, and faith must be understood as a possibility for the latter. Thus there is no reason why an ontological or existential analysis of human existence in general is not applicable to the believer as well as to the unbeliever. Men do not differ with regard to their ontological possibilities but only with regard to whether or not they realize their ontological possibilities. And Bultmann maintains that this is a possibility in fact in response to the Word of God in the kerygma of the Christian Church.

Bultmann does not intend that this exclude the possibility of revelation occurring elsewhere, as we shall see later in this study. However, given this perspective of the realization in fact of authentic existence, he does sound orthodox or traditional. In this context faith is defined in terms of obedience, surrendering our self-confidence and "resolving to trust in God alone, in the God who raises the dead (II Cor. 1:9) and who calls the things that are not into being (Rom. 4:17)."[44] In this act man abandons his past

---

42. *Mythology*, p. 76. See also Bultmann's review of *Christ without Myth* in *Journal of Religion*, XLII (July, 1962), 226.
43. *Kerygma and Myth* (London, 1957), p. 22.
44. *Ibid.*, p. 19.

in which he seeks to secure his life in the world of tangible realities. In opening up his heart to the grace of God his sins are forgiven and he is freed from his past. "In faith man understands himself ever anew. This new self-understanding can be maintained only as a continual response to the word of God which proclaims His action in Jesus Christ."[45]

Jaspers of course says, "Only this knowledge of our being grounded in transcendence can make us free in the world."[46] But for Bultmann this knowledge has reference to the encounter with God, which is not within but ever before me. The knowledge of faith is neither assent to propositions nor self-knowledge which recognizes the beyond in man as constitutive of his authentic existence. It is historical (*geschichtlich*) knowledge which is known only in relation to one's personal encounters in the world. Faith has its origin in a concrete event outside the self. The age of salvation has already dawned, and the life of the apocalyptic future is already present in the coming of Jesus.[47] This event is passed on to me in the proclamation of the Church, and faith is obedience to the specific act of God which is proclaimed here as an act for me.

> The New Testament proclaims that the freedom and the arbitrary nature of God's action is authenticated by the fact that he had acted decisively for all the world and for all time in the person of a concrete, historical man, *Jesus of Nazareth*. Through him everyone is addressed and asked if he is willing to hear God's message of forgiveness and grace here. In Jesus Christ the destiny of every man is decided. He is the *eschatological act of God*.[48]

Thus, faith for Paul, says Bultmann, is neither a psychic state nor a trust in God in general, not piety but a specific confession.

---

45. *Mythology*, p. 76.
46. *Myth*, p. 74.
47. *Kerygma and Myth* (London, 1957), p. 20.
48. Bultmann, *Essays Philosophical and Theological*, trans. James C. G. Grieg (London: S.C.M. Press, 1955), p. 85. Cited hereinafter as *Essays*.

Faith is knowledge not in the "sense of speculation about some historical or cosmic event, but rather a knowledge in which the man of faith also knows about himself and understands himself anew, in that he understands the saving act as a gift and himself as one to whom it has been given (I Cor. 3:12)."[49]

Bultmann's conception of faith then can be summarized by saying that it is a decision which is taken again and again in the face of God's gift, which confronts man in the proclamation of the Christian Church. It is a decision in which man understands himself free from past bondage to the world and living out of God's future. Man acknowledges himself as a recipient of that gift in which he understands himself anew, and in this way faith takes on the character of confession from within a particular historical tradition.

49. Schubert Ogden, ed., *Existence and Faith: Shorter Writings of Rudolf Bultmann* (New York: Meridian Books, 1960), p. 141. Cited hereinafter as *Existence*.

Philosophical and Christian Faith

Jaspers repeatedly says that philosophical faith does not eliminate or represent a substitute for religious faith. That is, he admits that the sphere of religion as community and worship may be indispensable to the majority of persons. But he does not have the same sympathy for theology, which exemplifies to him an exclusive approach to truth that makes communication between men impossible.

Jaspers is not proposing philosophical faith as an example of what has been traditionally referred to as "philosophical religion." Insofar as philosophical religion is said to be a religion which seeks to embrace all religions, it is said to ignore the historicity, the historical earnestness of religion. However, in criticizing what Jaspers calls orthodox faith he does seem to be demanding that Christian faith speak out of man's relation to the world in the dimension of general human experience and not from within a particular historical confession. In this sense Jaspers suggests that it is at least possible for theologians and philosophers to come to some agreement as to the method of clarification of the Encompassing without requiring uniformity in religious practice.[50]

If this suggestion is seen in the context of Jaspers' own method of clarifying the Encompassing, he may be understood to be suggesting that the indirect method of illuminating human existence, in such a way that it awakens to truth, would make possible openness to any number of religious traditions, since the myths and practices of these cults in themselves are not important. They gain

50. *Myth*, pp. 51 ff.

their importance only to the extent that they are vehicles which permit the awakening of the self to its being grounded in Transcendence. It is in this sense that the biblical faith continues to be of importance for Westerners.

Perhaps the majority of persons who read Jaspers' works will admit to sympathy with him at this point. Many religious thinkers have deplored the tendency in recent years on the part of both philosophers and theologians to separate philosophy and theology and to see them as essentially unrelated. And many persons have experienced in one way or another the demonic tendencies which are found when truth is absolutized in particular formulas through which the control of men is sought. Nevertheless, it is questionable whether the line between philosophy and theology or between faith and faith is as easily or as fruitfully overcome as Jaspers would tend to suggest.

The historicity of human existence as both Jaspers and Bultmann understand it speaks of man's choosing himself in the world. But if this is so, it is doubtful if the theologian who speaks out of a commitment of faith can actually transcend this particular situation in which he has made his decision of faith, as if to seek some common ground in the transcendent. That is, if I have responded to God whose Word I have heard from within the proclamation of a particular tradition, I may stand back from the decision in order to relate it to other dimensions of reality; but insofar as I seek to communicate the decision which I have made, I can only speak from within the context in which I have made it. This is not to deny the fact that the theologian may at times feel alienated from the community or tradition in which this commitment takes place. Neither does it mean that he must take up an attitude of exclusivism toward other claims to truth. But it does suggest that the decision is of such a nature that it affirms something and denies something else which might contradict it.

From this point of view the question arises whether Jaspers has really spoken of a decision of faith or whether philosophical faith is better understood as a rational clarification of that dimension in which faith may become a meaningful possibility. If the latter is the case, philosophical faith would seem to look to something like the Christian faith for its fulfilment, a suggestion that Jaspers does not wish to accept. Jaspers would probably say to us at this point that in philosophizing he is clarifying our way of being in order that we may affirm ourselves in relation to Transcendence. Yet immediately we do this, it seems, we affirm this relationship in some particular context, whereas philosophical faith must remain open to all traditions.

This problem is exemplified in the ambiguity that prevails whenever Jaspers attempts to characterize the finality and the openness of faith. Jaspers is certainly not unaware of the problem that is raised here. He realizes that Existenz must make a leap beyond the limits of reason as an ordinary cognizing act. In this sense philosophical faith, which is in reason, is more than reason. Philosophical faith is said by Jaspers to be "the fundamental source of that work by which man makes himself in an inner act as an individual before his Transcendence. . . ." Yet he completes this sentence, saying that the decision is "stimulated by tradition, but without any rationally defineable bond to any particular form."[51] We are asking whether there is a meaningful decision which does not take some particular form. Is it not the case that even Jaspers will have to depend upon a particular form of decision in order that it be meaningful?

On some occasions Jaspers seems to agree. He suggests, for instance, that the principles of philosophical faith are analogous to a creed and that the philosopher should say, "such faith, expressed in such propositions, strikes me as meaningful; I will venture to believe in this way. . . ." Yet in the same paragraph he says that the philosopher must say, "I do not know; I do not even know whether I believe."[52] Philosophical faith is intended by Jaspers to refer to the moment in which Existenz affirms itself in relation to Transcendence. Yet, because this can take no particular form,

51. *Reason*, p. 141.   52. *Wisdom*, p. 95.

faith speaks not of the commitment or the affirmation but of the way to it. And this way is one of openness, inquiry, incompleteness. It is this which Jaspers expresses in saying that "as long as man philosophizes, he knows he stands not in relation to the holy chain of 'witnesses to the Truth' . . . nor to that of atheism . . . ; but rather he is related to the chain of private men who openly search in freedom."[53]

Speaking as a Christian theologian, Bultmann is also able to acknowledge a community in which men are linked together in inquiry. He even refers to it as a community of the transcendent insofar as nihilists, atheists, mystics, and philosophers are linked together in a pilgrimage. He distinguishes this, however, from the community of the called, "in which are linked together those who have heard the Word with a believing ear and pass it on as they confess it."[54] Faith is able to understand the community of the transcendent as a community in search of God. But it looks to its community of the called as affirming a commitment which it must understand and proclaim so that its truth may be understood as a summons to others.

The problem for Jaspers is how to affirm Transcendence in a meaningful way apart from any particular form. The problem for Bultmann is how to speak of God from within the particular commitment of the Christian faith without losing Him in the finite and thus becoming a subject of Jaspers' criticism. If Bultmann wishes to make Christian faith something other than philosophical faith, he must clearly demonstrate its anchorage in history. Otherwise he will have a difficult time showing how Christian faith is other than a subjective experience whose meaning is called into question. At the same time, if he agrees with Jaspers that faith is not assent to doctrine, he must indicate how this can be maintained while presenting faith as a confession from within a particular historical tradition. Our investigation of this problem looks first to the idea of revelation, then to the problem of language and communication, and finally to the question of truth in faith.

53. *Reason*, p. 141.   54. *Essays*, p. 303.

II Revelation and Faith

General Revelation

Revelation means the disclosure of that which is otherwise hidden. It may refer to the disclosure of new information with which we were not previously acquainted, to an event in which we understand ourselves anew, or to some combination of both. And insofar as this revelation is said to be open to all men irrespective of their particular historical tradition, it may be spoken of as general revelation. Both Jaspers and Bultmann emphasize the event aspect of revelation, and both are open to the idea of a general revelation of Transcendence. Nevertheless, it is on the basis of a difference in views of revelation that Jaspers is able to distinguish philosophical faith from orthodox Christian faith and hence from Bultmann's conception of faith, which he associates with orthodoxy.

According to Jaspers, revelation may be understood in two ways. It may refer to the unique intervention of God in history at a given time and place. This is revelation in the sense of *Offenbarung* and according to him has nothing of the liberal spirit of a Lessing, a Kant, or a Goethe. But there is also revelation in the sense of *Offenbarwerden*, which refers to an inward act of the individual in which truth is disclosed independently of a particular time and place. It is in this latter liberal sense that philosophical faith speaks of revelation.[1]

Revelation in the orthodox sense, says Jaspers, means that God manifests Himself at a given place and time and only there. God is made to appear as an object in the world and men are sup-

1. *Myth*, p. 41.

posed to possess here the absoluteness of the godhead and to revere it on the basis of the authority of the tradition. Revelation in this sense is the immediate utterance of God, localized in time and valid for all men. In all of its utterances, its canonic writings, its creeds and so on, the revelation is conceived to be physically present.[2]

Jaspers rejects what he calls the orthodox view of revelation for three basic reasons. First, he does not wish to locate Transcendence in an observable object in the world. To identify God with the phenomena of the world is to objectify Him and thus to lose Him as the transcendent One. Religion, as Jaspers understands it, is bound up with a particular community of men, and it always embodies man's practical relation to the transcendent on the basis of something holy in the world which is distinguished from the unholy. Religion embodies its truth in tangible symbols and denounces the god of philosophy as a mere abstraction. But philosophy knows of no separate community, no existent invested with a sacred character and set apart from the world. Philosophy mistrusts the religious images of God and looks upon them as seductive idols. It maintains that all worldly images of God when mistaken for His reality only conceal Him. These images are properly understood as mere hints, metaphors of the transcendent God.[3] Thus, while philosophical faith does not deny that God can act as absolute Transcendence, it does insist that "all it can perceive is the actions, the sayings, and the experiences of human beings."[4]

Second, Jaspers maintains that orthodoxy arrests what is beyond the limits of comprehension. In its ready-made, self-sufficient dogmas, it resists all further development and clarification, turning the incomprehensible (*Unverständliche*) into an object of the understanding. The image that Jaspers has in mind, in saying this, is that of the individual or community which no longer listens and questions, which no longer in practice at least admits of the in-

2. *Perennial Scope*, p. 83.
3. *Ibid.*, pp. 75 ff.; *Wisdom*, pp. 48 ff.
4. *Myth*, p. 42.

comprehensibility of Being. Over against this, philosophical faith believes that we experience the incomprehensible in our knowledge of the world, of other men, and of ourselves. We experience the incomprehensible as something that is not fundamentally and absolutely incomprehensible but as something which is striving to be comprehended and is capable of endless clarification. Thus, man stands open to himself and the world in a movement of endless comprehension and not in the arrested state of one whose comprehension is full and complete.[5]

Third, Jaspers rejects orthodoxy's claim to an exclusive revelation. While he admits that absolute truth is something that is manifested in the immediate experience of the individual, he considers this experience falsified when it is made into a universal claim to truth for every man. "The absolute is not universal, but is historical in the impenetrable, self-illumined dynamism of the present act."[6] The result of all attempts to turn this individual experience of truth into a truth valid for all is deception, intolerance, and incapacity for communication with others. The claim to exclusive truth gives freedom to such impulses as the will to power, cruelty, and the impulse to destroy. And these impulses are justified on the basis of the truth that man claims to possess. Contrary to this, philosophical faith rejects all forms of exclusivism and recognizes various avenues to God. "It recognizes that the way to God is possible also without Christ, and that the Asians can find it without the Bible."[7] Jaspers does not mean that one must make a synthesis of all religions in the manner of the Enlightenment. But he does mean that one should concentrate on the *pro-me* of revelation, the becoming of God as the absolute in my particular historical experience. On this basis one can make claims to truth only in oneself and cannot create from this a universally valid truth.[8]

Jaspers leaves us in no doubt concerning his opinion of the idea

5. *Ibid.*, pp. 38–39.
6. *Perennial Scope*, p. 90.
7. *Myth*, p. 46.
8. *Perennial Scope*, pp. 112–113.

of revelation as it is conceived in the so-called orthodox sense. He maintains, however, that we can speak meaningfully of revelation in a different sense. Revelation for Jaspers is *Offenbarwerden*, a view of the disclosure of truth which he believes to have reached its deepest level in the thought of Kierkegaard.[9] The *Offenbarwerden* of truth occurs in an inner act of man in which he becomes aware of the true possibilities of his being and his relation to Transcendence. This illumination of the self and Transcendence is distinguished from all empirical forms of understanding in that it cannot be grounded in objective knowledge. It does not refer to something which is manifested in a community, but only to the individual act in which one becomes aware of one's potential selfhood. Here, one stumbles upon the mystery that in the act of self-creation, the self is received as a gift from beyond. When man makes himself, so to speak, he becomes acquainted with Transcendence.

In Jasper's understanding of "revelation," then, the transcendent Reality reveals itself not in some object in the world, but in the inner consciousness of man. The disclosure of truth occurs in the moment of individual existence, when man confronts simultaneously his authentic self and the transcendent Other. This understanding of revelation or illumination has certain mystical characteristics, and yet Jaspers continually separates it from a type of mysticism in which one flees from the finite world and communication with others. On the contrary, the inner act in which one catches a glimpse of Eternity is said to come through the world and in communication with others.

Offenbarwerden is tied up with reflection. It is in reflecting upon the world and himself in the world that man awakens to the presence of Transcendence. The world and everything in it is a mystery which philosophy seeks to illuminate and bring into consciousness. It is the symbol or myth which "preserves" this mystery for us. Otherwise it would be lost in a void while we sought to

9. *Wahrheit*, pp. 540 ff.; *Myth*, pp. 41 ff.

gain ourselves in the definite knowledge of the finite world. In transcending the limits of the objective structure of the symbol, we are turned inward upon ourselves; the objective structure is suspended and becomes transparent to Transcendence in our inner experience of freedom and authentic selfhood.[10]

Revelation in this sense does not refer to something that can be definitely known but to that which can be apprehended only indirectly through the world. Thus it cannot refer to something that happened once and for all in some particular period of time. The Being of Transcendence must be at any time or place newly and freely grasped.[11] In my individual historicity, I experience the presence of Being as that which I have always known, but which can never be bound to a worldly form.[12]

The idea of revelation then does not imply for Jaspers a flight from the rational world. Rather, man ascends through the world to the presence of Transcendence. He moves within the horizons of thought, questioning and seeking in communication with others, coming to rest in no stable knowledge of the world. Man researches in the sciences, seeking to raise his experience into consciousness, to transform it into knowledge. He questions his being and potentialities in the light of the words and maxims of history which he encounters. He seeks fundamental knowledge, the ordering of his knowing consciousness.[13] But this world in which man lives and works is not self-explanatory. At the limits of the knowledge of objects and the self who is the subject of knowledge, man comes up against a boundary, the limit of human understanding, and here he founders. At this limit, the manifestation of transcendent Being is possible. In the acknowledgment of his freedom from the objective world and hence his possibilities beyond it, the individual stands open to Transcendence, the source of his potentiality. The world through which he has plunged is read as a cipher, the secret script of the transcendent Reality. Transcendence is

---

10. *Truth*, pp. 37 ff.
11. *Wahrheit*, p. 788.

12. *Truth*, p. 65.
13. *Ibid.*, pp. 70–71.

unveiled, not in the secure categories of the world, but in the inner experience in which man becomes himself.

Offenbarwerden is immediate; it requires no intermediary being. God is accessible to man not through some external authority but through the orientation toward God that lies at the source of human existence. The individual is not referred to an other, but to himself. This is a truth which Jaspers finds embodied in the Christian religion. The spirit of Christ is said to belong to each individual. "It is the *pneuma*, i.e. the spirit of an enthusiasm surging upward to the supra-sensory. It is also the openness to one's own suffering as a road to transcendence; he who has taken the cross upon himself can ascertain the authentic in failure."[14] According to Jaspers, the "Christ in me" and the God-given *nobilitas ingenita* mean the same thing, the actuality of the Divine in man, which man either follows or betrays. That is, it is not simply a natural possession but must be realized, chosen in every situation.[15]

However, this does not mean for Jaspers that man must apprehend the redeeming Christ outside himself by realizing the spirit of Christ in himself. There is no exclusive bond between the Christ in me and the historical Jesus. Jesus as the God-man is a myth, and man cannot arbitrarily limit demythologizing at this point.[16] Jesus, like all other worldly realities, is but a cipher of transcendent Being. Man is not bound to him but stands in an independent relation to God in his freedom. In his own historicity man is capable of a relation to God that requires no intermediary.[17]

If Bultmann's conception of revelation may be said to emphasize the coming up against God who encounters me as Thou, calling me to choose my authentic self, Jaspers' conception of revelation emphasizes the awakening to my authentic selfhood at the end of philosophical reflection. It is the awaking to the presence of truth, which, if hidden, is always present for man who is free from bondage to the world. Revelation is more like the switching on of a

14. *Perennial Scope*, p. 105.   16. *Perennial Scope*, pp. 104–106.
15. *Myth*, pp. 50–51.   17. *Wisdom*, p. 47.

light in a room that I had forgotten than an encounter with a divine Thou who stands over against me making demands of me. *Offenbarwerden* is not graceless; that is, it is not something that I create out of myself. But its grace is one which is continuous with my being.

As a theologian Bultmann is particularly sensitive to the nineteenth-century tendency to replace the revelation of God with human discovery and shares with Sören Kierkegaard and Karl Barth the concern that the "infinite qualitative difference between God and man" be maintained. However, he is also aware that this reaction to nineteenth-century thought may result in a failure to treat adequately the biblical understanding of revelation in nature and history, a criticism which Emil Brunner has brought against Barth.[18] Like Barth, Bultmann understands God to be unknowable apart from his revelation of himself. But unlike Barth, he points to a general or natural revelation of God in nature, history, and conscience which makes possible at least a negative or indirect knowledge of God.

Bultmann's thought is very similar to that of Martin Luther at this point. Like Luther, he rejects natural theology in its classical sense; that is, he rejects the idea that a definite knowledge of God is possible on the basis of rational inference from the rational order. Bultmann rejects natural theology in this sense not only because of the philosophical criticism of it, but primarily because it ignores the fact that the one and only approach to God is through faith. If one accepts the knowledge of God as set forth in traditional natural theology, God's transcendence is forgotten, and God is known in the manner of the world. For example, in the Stoic tradition God is understood as the immanent energy by which the natural world is sustained and as the world-reason which manifests itself in the order and beauty of the world. However, when one understands God in faith as that which transcends the natural

18. Emil Brunner, *Revelation and Reason*, trans. Olive Wyon (Philadelphia: Westminster, 1946, and London: S.C.M. Press, 1947), pp. 79–80.

order, the only real knowledge of God comes at God's initiative, in His revelation of Himself. Similarly, Bultmann rejects the form of natural theology in which a knowledge of God is maintained on the basis of a religious a priori. Here the distinction between God and man is diminished, and revelation and faith are reduced to the proceedings of the Spirit and the consciousness.[19]

Also, like Luther, Bultmann acknowledges a general revelation of God and hence a general knowledge of God. According to Luther, there is a twofold knowledge of God, one general and available to all men and one particular and available only to those who participate in faith in Jesus Christ. The general knowledge of God is not based on man's discovery of Him, however, but upon God's revelation of Himself in creation. God is apprehended in and through creation and not from behind it on the basis of man's rational inference. God encounters man in the natural order, the same God who meets him in Christ. However, man does not rightly recognize God in His general revelation and closes himself off from Him, seeking his own security in himself and in the world in which he lives. In other words, man perverts God's general revelation, and the general knowledge of God, perverted by sin, becomes a form of idolatry.[20]

The similarity between Luther's and Bultmann's thought becomes apparent when we attempt to say what Bultmann means by the general revelation of God in creation. Bultmann maintains that there is a knowledge of God available to all men which is not dependent upon the particular revelation in Jesus Christ. God's revelation in creation makes it possible for all men to have a concept of God, although from the viewpoint of Christian faith, this knowledge is distinguished from "acquaintance" with God in faith. Bultmann refers to this knowledge, based on God's revelation in creation, as man's knowledge of his own limitations and

---

19. Bultmann, *Glauben und Verstehen*, I (Tübingen: J.C.B. Mohr [Paul Siebeck], 1961), 294 ff. Cited hereinafter as *G.V.*, I.
20. Philip Watson, *Let God Be God* (London: Epworth, 1947, and Philadelphia: Mullenberg, 1949), pp. 73–74.

insignificance or as a knowledge of God in advance of the revelation in Jesus Christ.[21]

Bultmann's references to a general revelation of God are frequent, but they are always made from within the perspective of the Christian faith. That is, he does not step outside of faith and observe it from a distance, so to speak. He can speak of general revelation only as he sees it from within the revelation in Christ. Thus, while Bultmann maintains that man does have a knowledge of God in his understanding of himself and his limitations and that if man kept this knowledge open "creation would speak as God's Word for him," he also says that the Christian faith believes that man does not keep this knowledge open, that he twists this negative knowledge into a positive knowledge, and that creation becomes mute for him.[22]

> For the revelation in Christ is not the first. Man could already have known God earlier. From the beginning, the "word" was the "light" of men. . . . Naturally, this light, this knowledge about God is not a cosmological or theological theory, but rather is an understanding of oneself through acknowledging the Creator. But the world has displaced this knowledge by the knowledge of what it itself does and has. . . . In a similar way, Paul teaches (in Stoic terminology) that man should have recognized the world as creation and honored God as God, although, in fact, he has done exactly the opposite.

> Thus there is a "natural revelation," or, at least, there *was* one. But it is not something that simply lies before one's eyes, nor is the knowledge of it a knowledge of the world, a theistic view of God. Rather it is a knowledge by man of himself, an understanding of himself as a creature and thus an honoring of God. This possibility has especially been given to the Jew through the law, in which he daily encounters God's claim and by which he is daily led to see that he does not exist by and

21. *Mythology*, p. 52; *Essays*, pp. 91, 94, 114.   22. *Essays*, pp. 114–115.

for himself, but that his being is limited by the claim under which he stands.

But man misunderstands himself and puts himself in the place of God. And every man comes out of a history that is governed by this misunderstanding. . . . There is another possibility only if it is given to him to come into his present from somewhere other than from a lie and from sin. And that this possibility *is* given is what is proclaimed in the message of Christ.[23]

This awareness of the general revelation of God and the sinfulness of man makes possible both the contact and the conflict between the Christian faith and other claims to truth. Bultmann is not satisfied with a simple dismissal of natural theology, although he looks on all expressions of faith outside the Christian faith as unbelief. According to Bultmann, the fact that one understands the Christian proclamation suggests some prior knowledge of God. The man of faith looks back to his old self and knows that he has already rejected God's revelation, that he has rejected the opportunity to fulfil himself in relation to God and has chosen to secure himself in the world.[24]

Bultmann also acknowledges that man speaks of belief in God outside the Christian faith. And while he considers this to be unbelief from the point of view of faith, he nevertheless recognizes here a knowledge of the self which is dependent on God's activity.[25] Similarly, Bultmann observes the relationship between the philosophical and theological understanding of man. Philosophy and theology talk about the same man, but theology sees man through the eyes of faith. Thus faith and unbelief are not talking about two different beings but of one whom faith considers to be not the natural man but the converted sinner.[26]

The Christian faith, then, has contact with all claims to truth

23. *Existence*, pp. 82–83. Compare with the long passage from Luther cited by Watson, *Let God Be God*, pp. 73–74.
24. *G.V.*, I pp. 295–296.
25. *Ibid.*, pp. 300–301.   26. *Ibid.*, pp. 305 ff.

on the basis of man's understanding of his existence in relation to God. Because faith looks upon other claims to truth as unbelief, it acknowledges that God is already revealing Himself to man. All men have an advance relationship to God in what Augustine has called the restless heart. "Man's life is moved by the search for God because it is always moved, consciously or unconsciously, by the question about his own personal existence. The question of God and the question of myself are identical."[27] These questions are identical not because theology is identical with philosophy or psychology but because man's understanding of himself is dependent on his relation to God. This relationship is not founded upon some hidden or revealed *deus in nobis,* but upon God's initiative in revealing Himself to man in creation.

However, the Christian faith conflicts with all other claims to truth when it refers to them as unbelief. It acknowledges the possibility of a general knowledge of God, but maintains that because of man's sin this possibility is closed off and God's Word in creation becomes mute. If man would remain in open inquiry and expectation, God's Word would address him. But, in fact, man rebels against this openness to the future of God and in attempting to construct his own image of God, loses Him. God reveals Himself everywhere and always, but because of his sin man does not have the freedom to remain open to this revelation. This freedom, according to Bultmann, comes only in faith's response to the proclamation of God's Word of forgiveness in the event of Jesus Christ.

The Christian faith, then, in accepting God's general revelation of Himself does not mean to suggest that the believer can return to a stage of open inquiry and thus find God. Faith says that this inquiry is completed by man in an answer which represents unbelief to Christianity. But faith does, according to Bultmann, acknowledge the possibility of man's knowledge of God apart from Christ, and consequently it holds man responsible for his unbelief. The revelation of God in nature and history reveals our

27. *Mythology,* p. 53.

limitations and teaches us that we do not possess the revelation. It directs us into the attitude of the man who knows that he can only receive. Thus it constantly refers us to the revelation of God in Christ. Only in this way is it revelation for us, "and that means that, apart from Christ, it is not revelation for us. But when we do start from Christ, the whole of the world in nature and history can receive the illumination of revelation."[28]

28. *Essays*, p. 118.

Special Revelation

Special revelation refers to the unique occurrence of revelation in history and the sense in which the Christian faith maintains a vital connection with this event. According to Jaspers, special revelation results in the dogmatic claim that God has assumed an objective form in history. What is only a cipher of Being becomes an objectification of Being, and what is true for one person's history is made into a truth valid for all people.

Jaspers agrees that Transcendence is revealed to man in his particular historical tradition, but he sees no necessary connection between the particular historical facts of that tradition and the transcendent truth. According to Jaspers, revelation occurs when the world of objects becomes a cipher of the transcendent Reality. But since objectivity is suspended in this experience, there is no necessary relation between the object and the revelatory moment. All the world is a potential cipher of Transcendence, including the event of Jesus; but the worldly reality ought never to be spoken of in such a way that it may be said to contain Transcendence or be identified with it.[29]

Jaspers is willing to admit then that God addresses man in the cipher of the God-man. He acknowledges the validity of the speculations on this cipher, especially those undertaken by Nicolaus Cusanus. But he distinguishes this appreciation of the Christian tradition from religious faith in revelation, which, according to him, does not refer to Jesus as a cipher but as the Reality (*Wirklichkeit*) of God, which is and was present in space and time as

29. *Truth*, p. 76.

the worldly reality (*Realität*).[30] Once the revelation has been spoken, says Jaspers, once it assumes a mundane form, it deteriorates into finiteness and even trivial rationality, and its meaning is perverted. Philosophical faith "repudiates an objective redemptive history conceived as an absolute event and as a prerequisite of salvation for all men," but "it accepts this history as a myth."[31] It, like all other myths, has its value in proportion to its existential content.

> As in the case of other myths, the validity of this [Christian] one must be tested existentially, and judged on the basis of the strength that emanates from its language, the truth that arises from it in the reality of life. Liberalism recognizes faith in revelation, including belief in the truth of the redemptive history as a possible truth valid for him who believes it—in so far as the believer does not, by his deeds or words, draw consequences destructive to the freedom of men who find themselves directly before God, nor attempt to coerce others by violent means.[32]

Jaspers' attitude toward the once-happenedness (*Einmaligkeit*) of the Christian revelation is illuminated in his study of the life of Jesus, as presented in *The Great Philosophers*. In this study his aim is to bring the reader into a relationship with the humanity of Jesus of Nazareth. The ultimate purpose of such a venture is that we might become ourselves by contemplating that which is eternal.[33] He has explained this attitude toward Jesus in another place, saying:

> The philosopher, as opposed to the critical-historical skeptic, regards Jesus as a historical figure, and sees in Jesus' faith the same calm determination which the philosopher seeks, and the same uncertainty with respect to God's will, which the philoso-

---

30. Jaspers, *Philosophische Glaube angesichts der Offenbarung* (Munich: R. Piper Verlag, 1962), pp. 251–254. Cited hereinafter as *Offenbarung*.
31. *Myth*, p. 47.
32. *Ibid*.
33. Jaspers, *The Great Philosophers*, ed. H. Arendt and trans. R. Manheim (New York: Harcourt, Brace and World, 1962), pp. vii–x, 74.

pher experiences. To him, Jesus, a man, represents questioning of God, obedience to God, search for God—i.e., to know God's intentions—a search he carries on although he is already secure in God. To him Jesus represents the overcoming of all human rigidities and presumptions, a breakthrough to truthfulness and love that knew no bounds, one of the great men who have been crucial in determining the course of philosophy. But nowhere is the direct word of God to be found. This conception of Jesus is that of the synoptics (prior to the later editions); it is not that of the Gospel according to St. John.[34]

Jaspers' study of the life of Jesus, which is untouched by recent New Testament scholarship, sets out to arrive at a portrait of Jesus which he considers to be "clearly discernible through the veil of tradition."[35] The philosopher in producing such a study is said to be seeking inspiration from the experience of Jesus. In communication with Jesus and other figures such as Socrates, Buddha, and Confucius, man might become aware of himself and his potential Existenz.

> For philosophy they are men. As men they must have their particular traits of character, their limitations; because they are historical, they cannot have universal validity for all. There are four of them; no one can be taken exclusively and alone. Where one of them is absolutized as the one and only truth, it means that believers have divested his image of all natural humanity. . . . Our philosophical attitude toward them is this: We are moved by what they have in common, because we stand with them in the situation of being men. None of them can be indifferent to us. Each one is a question addressed to us that leaves us no peace.[36]

For Jaspers the lives of such men are "beacons by which to gain an orientation."[37] They cannot be authorities in themselves but only as they direct us to transcendent Reality. Philosophical faith

---

34. *Myth*, p. 82.
35. *The Great Philosophers*, p. 74.
36. *Ibid.*, p. 105.
37. *Ibid.*

"looks on all formulated and written philosophy only as preparation or recollection, only as inspiration or confirmation."[38] The
only other possibility that Jaspers sees is one in which a particular
history or tradition is made exclusive. That is, either one looks
upon history as an inspiration or stimulus, or one absolutizes a
particular history and thus reduces Transcendence to the level of
worldly knowledge.

In contrast to Jaspers' tendency to dissolve any real connection
between revelation and particular historical events, the New Testament maintains that faith has an indissoluble relationship with
the historical event, Jesus of Nazareth. Jaspers interprets this to
mean that revelation is identified with an objective event. But Bultmann replies that faith does not identify an objective historical
event with revelation. Rather, it believes that God's revelation
takes place within this event. Revelation for Bultmann is not
simply the communication of objective knowledge. It is an occurrence in the life of man in which he responds to the event of Jesus
who died and was raised for him.[39] In this occurrence man comes
to a new understanding of himself; *"everything has been revealed
insofar as man's eyes are opened concerning his own existence and
he is once again able to understand himself."*[40] According to Bultmann it is this that Martin Luther meant in saying, "Thus, in going
out of himself, God brings it about that we go into ourselves; and
through knowledge of him, he brings us to a knowledge of ourselves."[41]

Bultmann's exposition of the Christian revelation brings together
two factors which he considers to be inseparable. First, there is
the present encounter with God in which my understanding of myself in relation to God is altered. It is here that we find Bultmann's

---

38. *Perennial Scope*, p. 10.   39. *Existence*, pp. 74–75.
40. *Ibid.*, p. 85.
41. *Existence*, pp. 85–86. In the same context Bultmann cites Karl Barth's
saying: "To hear God's word does not mean to wander in the remote realm
of metaphysics, but rather at long last to come to oneself, to learn to see
oneself, to be revealed to oneself as one really is" (*Existence*, p. 301, n. 11).

relation to Kierkegaard and consequently to Jaspers. This is an event which takes place only in my life in the present and can never be identified with an objective event in time. But second, this present encounter is, according to Bultmann, bound up in an indissoluble way to the past event in which Jesus of Nazareth is understood as the eschatological event in faith. If Jaspers does not always see clearly the first aspect of revelation in Bultmann's thought, other critics do not always see the second. For Bultmann the present and the past come together as one in faith's response to the proclamation of the Christian Church.[42]

Bultmann is well aware of the limitations of revelation in which God becomes an object in the world. It is this which gives the impetus to his program of demythologizing. The mythological element of Christianity, which objectifies revelation, is interpreted by Bultmann so that its essential meaning as a possibility of human existence is laid bare. But Bultmann is also aware of the limitations of nineteenth-century theology which tended on occasion to forget the historical roots of revelation. It is the kerygma which proclaims Jesus Christ as the ever present Word of God, which sets an end to our old world and brings in the new. However, "The Now of the kerygma (2 Cor. 6:2) is not purely fortuitous, but identical with the advent of Jesus and his passion."[43] It is not that the facts of the past are recalled in their worldly actuality or that one encounters human existence and its interpretation in the past. Rather, in the recollection of the kerygma, the events of the past are re-presented in such a way that within them God's Word may encounter me, demanding a decision from me.

Bultmann's attempt to bring together the personal encounter of God with man in the moment and the particular history of Jesus of Nazareth has been met by many objections. Some of these may be explained away as examples of misunderstanding, but others

42. *Kerygma und Mythos*, VI/1 (Hamburg: Herbert Reich Evangelischer Verlag, 1963), pp. 26–27.
43. *Kerygma and Myth* (London, 1957), p. 115.

often suggest problem areas for Bultmann's thought as well as the thought of his contemporaries. Most of these objections have avoided the extremes of Helmut Thielicke, who says that Bultmann reduces revelation to self-consciousness, and Jaspers, who accuses him of objectifying it.[44] They have tended rather to suggest that Bultmann treats inadequately the meaning of the past event for the present encounter. Julius Schniewind, for instance, rejects Thielicke's criticism and maintains that Bultmann has never denied a relationship between the "now" of the revelatory moment and the event which occurred in the Palestinian world in the first century. Nevertheless, he does believe that history is not treated adequately by Bultmann.[45]

H. P. Owen makes a similar criticism in declaring that the distinction that Bultmann makes between *Historie* and *Geschichte* cannot be maintained, and Giovanni Miegge says that the Jesus of history is dissolved "almost without remainder, into the Christ of faith," that Jesus' significance is found by Bultmann not in the what of his life but only in its "that," that he was.[46] Ian Henderson speaks of the "subordinate role" of Jesus, and John Macquarrie maintains that Bultmann speaks at times as if historical factuality were quite irrelevant.[47] Yet in response to these critics Schubert Ogden has declared that Bultmann is being misunderstood, that he has always maintained the continuity between the Jesus of history and the Christ of the kerygma.[48]

There does in fact seem to be very little reason to question whether or not Bultmann has maintained *some* continuity between the historical Jesus and the early Christian kerygma. Here one

---

44. *Ibid.*, pp. 76, 148, 154; *Myth*, pp. 76 ff.

45. *Kerygma and Myth* (London, 1957), pp. 79 ff.

46. H. P. Owen, *Revelation and Existence: A Study in the Theology of Rudolf Bultmann* (Cardiff: Univ. of Wales Press, 1957, and Mystic, Conn.: Lawrence Verry, 1964), pp. 112–115. Giovanni Miegge, *Gospel and Myth in the Thought of Rudolf Bultmann* (London: Lutterworth Press, 1960, and Richmond, Va.: John Knox Press, 1960), pp. 126 ff.

47. Ian Henderson, *Myth in the New Testament* (London: S.C.M. Press, 1952), p. 49; Macquarrie, *The Scope of Demythologizing*, p. 91.

48. Ogden, *Christ without Myth*, pp. 81 ff.

can sympathize with Ogden's attempt to defend Bultmann. According to Bultmann there would be no kerygma if there had been no historical Jesus. Jesus in this sense is the presupposition of the kerygma. However, *that* Jesus lived and died is apparently the only thing of importance in this connection. Bultmann resists conversation regarding the what and how of Jesus' life, saying that it was only the "that" of his life which was essential to the preaching of Paul and John.[49]

In a similar manner Bultmann makes it clear that existential interpretation is based on certain objective events in time which are available to the eyes of scientific historical research. Without a basis in history, revelation would, according to him, result in a mere picture of fantasy.[50] Because of this he does not resist all attempts to portray the historical Jesus. While he claims that the Synoptic Gospels do not suffice as sources for a reconstruction of Jesus' life, that they tell us nothing of his inner being, they do, he says, let us know enough of Jesus' work to make certain traits of his life visible. According to Bultmann, one might with caution suggest, for example, that Jesus was an exorcist, that he broke the sabbath law, that he had fellowship with outcasts, that he was not an ascetic like John, and that he proclaimed the eschatological message of the immanent rule of God.[51] But this knowledge does not, Bultmann maintains, have much to do with the present encounter with the Christ of the kerygma. Scientific historical (*historisch*) research is relevant only insofar as it is able to confirm with some probability the *that* of the kerygma, that is, insofar as it acts against any skepticism of the historicity of Jesus. The present historical (*geschichtlich*) encounter with the Christ of the kerygma is not an encounter with the objective historical picture

---

49. Bultmann, *Das Verhältnis der urchristlichen Christusbotschaft zum historischen Jesus* (Heidelberg: Carl Winter Universitätsverlag, 1962), pp. 8 ff. Cited hereinafter as *Heidelberg Lecture.* See also Bultmann, *Theology of the New Testament,* I (New York: Scribner's, 1951), 3.

50. *Kerygma und Mythos,* VI/1, p. 23.

51. *Heidelberg Lecture,* pp. 11 ff.; *Kerygma and Myth* (London, 1957), p. 117.

of Jesus but with the Christ proclaimed as God's Word, and historical research can never prove its legitimacy.[52]

Hermann Diem tells us that Reformation theology found the unity between the Jesus of history and the Christ of faith in faith's decision before the proclamation of the Church.[53] In the kerygma of the Church, Christ becomes the eschatological event for the believer. It is in a similar manner that Bultmann would seek this continuity. The kerygma which presupposes the "that" of the historical Jesus takes the place of Jesus for us and re-presents his coming as the present eschatological event for us. The kerygma transforms the "once" of the historical Jesus into the "once for all" and announces the decisive eschatological event as an event for us in the present.

In the kerygma the *historisch* event is proclaimed as the eschatological event. Jesus is proclaimed as Lord, and in faith an end is set to the old self and the new self is received as a gift. And since it is the Church through the kerygma that makes possible the repetition of this event, faith in Christ is at the same time faith in the Church as the bearer of the kerygma.

> If it is the case that the kerygma proclaims Jesus as the Christ, as the eschatological event, if it claims that Christ is present in it, then it has put itself in the place of the historical Jesus; it represents him. There is then no faith in Christ which is not at the same time faith in the Church as the bearer of the kerygma, i.e., in the terminology of dogmatics, faith in the Holy Spirit. But faith in the Church is at the same time faith in Jesus Christ, a faith which the historical Jesus did not demand. . . . If it is true that the Church in its kerygma represents the historical Jesus, if faith in Christ is at the same time faith in the Church or faith in the Holy Spirit, . . . then one

---

52. *Heidelberg Lecture*, pp. 13–14.
53. Hermann Diem, "The Earthly Jesus and the Christ of Faith," in *Kerygma and History*, ed. and trans. C. Braaten and K. Harrisville (Nashville: Abingdon, 1962), p. 198. See *Heidelberg Lecture*, p. 25.

can say that faith in the Church as the bearer of the kerygma is the Easter faith which consists of the faith that Jesus Christ is present in the kerygma. It is often said, and usually in a critical sense, that according to my interpretation of the kerygma Jesus has risen into the kerygma. I accept this way of expressing it. It is entirely correct, assuming that it is correctly understood. It presupposes that the kerygma itself is an eschatological event. And it means that Jesus is actually present in the kerygma, that it is *his* word that encounters the hearer in the kerygma.[54]

The Church's proclamation itself is a historical event which may attract the attention of scientific historical research. But it becomes the revelatory event, the eschatological event, only in the moment when an end is set to my old world and the new is ushered in. Jesus is present as the Christ in the proclamation of the Church when God's Word addresses me here, when I, living in the world, am freed from bondage to it. If the present encounter with the Word of God is separated from history it loses its ground in time, and faith becomes an otherworldly mysticism at best. But if the present encounter is reduced to what can be found in scientific historical investigation, the transcendent dimension of this event is lost. Both the historical and the transcendent aspects of revelation are maintained only when one leaps, so to speak, from *Historie* into *Geschichte* and finds that the *geschichtlich* encounter has its basis in God's act within *Historie*. The Christian faith maintains that this has occurred in the event of Jesus and that it occurs again and again in the preaching of the Church.

In this manner Bultmann believes himself to have avoided the problem raised by his critics. That is, he does not believe that he has destroyed the continuity between the historical Jesus and the Christ of faith. And to a certain extent he is certainly right. However, he does not really seem to grasp the problem that underlies

---

54. *Heidelberg Lecture*, pp. 26–27.

the concern of his more cautious critics. Recently, for instance, he has replied to H. P. Owen, saying that "the danger that the hearing will be understood as a merely subjective action of the hearer is avoided if the preaching is so understood that in it the eschatological event (Jesus Christ) is being fulfilled constantly in the present."[55] Yet this is not answering the real question. Bultmann has already told us that Jesus is present in the proclamation of the Church.[56] But the problem is that this event seems to have no meaning if the what and how of Jesus' life are in all cases expendable.

Bultmann indicates at one point that we have in the New Testament the picture of Christ which makes God not only hidden but also revealed.[57] But if this picture cannot be said to be in some way actually grounded in Jesus it is difficult to see how it would be more than the announcement of a general truth. On the other hand, if it is grounded only in Jesus' "that," it is difficult to see what meaning the event has, what it brings to expression. It is, I believe, this apparent indifference to the what of Jesus' life that lies behind the question of Macquarrie and others. Until this is clarified, Bultmann's departure from Jaspers' more negative approach to God's revelation will be seriously impaired. God may be little more than the silence at the end of reflection, or he may be identified with an arbitrary and hence unreal assertion.

55. Bultmann, "Reply," in *The Theology of Rudolf Bultmann*, ed. C. W. Kegley (New York: Harper and Row, 1966), p. 261.
56. *Heidelberg Lecture*, p. 27; *Myth*, p. 70.
57. *Existence*, p. 33.

Exclusivism of Revelation

Much of Jaspers' criticism of religious faith has its basis in what he calls the exclusivism of revelation. According to him, absolute truth is historical, that is, present only in the moment of individual existence. Transcendence is present in the world but only in the inner experience of man. Thus it stands beyond the categories of human conceptualization which are necessary to universally valid truths. Yet, he maintains, Christian theologians do not speak of *my* way of truth but of *the* way to truth. They turn what is absolute for them into a universally valid truth. The absolute historical truth which is known only in faith and has no certainty or guarantee in the world is replaced by superstition in which Transcendence is bound to objectivity and universality.[58]

According to Jaspers, the binding of revelation to objective categories, and hence the reducing of transcendent truth to the level of objective truth, results in exclusivism and intolerance. The claim to certainty replaces the uncertainty of faith. The Christian believer counts all persons to be lost who live before or without the coming of Christ. The Christian thinks of adherents to other religions as heathen and seeks to force belief where it is not accepted voluntarily. This results in self-deception, intolerance, and the incapacity for communication with others. It is this attitude which Jaspers holds responsible for the breakdown in discussion between philosophers and theologians.[59]

Philosophical faith rejects all claims to an exclusive truth while acknowledging the validity of the absolute truth of historical reve-

---

58. *Perennial Scope*, pp. 89 ff.
59. *Myth*, pp. 45 ff.; *Perennial Scope*, pp. 89 ff.

lation. Absolute truth is not universally valid, but is "historical in the impenetrable, self-illumined dynamism of the present act."[60] That is, truth is absolute in individual experience although every formulation of it is relative.

> It [absolute truth] is profoundly unknown, much as can be known and said through it. Nothing can take its place, it is always unique and yet it may serve others not only as an orientation, but as a prototype by which to recognize something of their own which differs from it in its historical manifestation and yet coincides with it in the light of eternity. That which is historically, existentially true is indeed absolute, but this does not mean that the expression or manifestation of it is a truth for all. . . . The absoluteness of historical truth implies the relativity of every formulation of it, and of all its historically finite manifestations. Universally valid statements can be based only upon relative standpoints and methods. Formulable faith contents must not be treated like universally true propositions; the absolute awareness of truth in faith is something fundamentally different from the comprehension of the universal validity of scientifically true propositions, which are always particular.[61]

There is then only one transcendent truth, but there are manifold manifestations and formulations of it. Each of these formulations is relative insofar as it is conposed of finite words and actions. Truth is not contained in the human form itself but only in the revelatory moment when Existenz actually confronts the beyond. This truth cannot be contained in one formulation or a combination of them but is known only when we pass beyond all formulations to the truth itself. And this takes place in individual reflection and in communication with others.

Thus, when Jaspers surveys history, he does not find its center or its axial period in the appearance of Jesus of Nazareth, for this

60. *Perennial Scope*, p. 90.   61. *Ibid.*, pp. 90–91.

would make the meaning of human existence dependent upon a particular manifestation of truth. It would universalize that which is valid only for believing Christians. Jaspers locates the axial period of history between 800 B.C. and 200 B.C., the time when men of various traditions became conscious of their being as a whole, of their possibilities and limitations, and strove for liberation and redemption. Confucius and Lao-tse were living in China, and all the schools of Chinese philosophy came into being. India produced the Upanishads and Buddha, and ran the whole gamut of philosophical possibilities. In Iran, Zarathustra appeared, and in Palestine, the prophets. Greece witnessed the appearance of Homer, Parmenides, Heraclitus, Plato, and others. During this period men independently and simultaneously became conscious of their limitedness and inquired after Being as a whole.

> What is new about this age, in all three areas of the world, is that man becomes conscious of Being as a whole, of himself and his limitations. He experiences the terror of the world and his own powerlessness. He asks radical questions. Face to face with the void he strives for liberation and redemption. By consciously recognising his limits he sets himself the highest goals. He experiences absoluteness in the depths of selfhood and in the lucidity of transcendence.[62]

This period of universal history was characterized by reflection. Communication took place between persons with various experiences and thoughts. Man was no longer inclosed within himself but became uncertain of himself and thus open to new and boundless possibilities. "Together with his world and his own self, Being becomes sensible to man, but not with finality: the question remains."[63] In this way men, who are separated by particular traditions and manifestations of truth, can be seen to be at one in the uncertainty of existence which gives rise to the quest for the One that lies beyond all finite formulations. That which is the origin

---

62. *Origin*, p. 2.   63. *Ibid.*, p. 3.

and goal of life is only ambiguously present in the particular
formulations of particular people.

It is this which leads Jaspers to say that men cannot be unified
on the basis of the contents of faith in *Offenbarung*. Man's unity
with others is based on the universal quest for truth and the
knowledge of oneself. It is, according to Jaspers, man's awareness
of his limitations and his openness to others in inquiry that is the
best remedy against the narrow exclusivism that makes a creed
into a truth valid for all.[64] He agrees that man experiences absolute truth in a particular tradition but maintains that man must
nevertheless remain open to other traditions so that in communication with them he might understand himself.

The question Jaspers raises concerning the exclusivism of revelation or the relation of the particular claim to truth to the various
other claims is a troublesome one for Christian theologians, and
Bultmann is no exception. That it does present a problem to the
interpreter of Bultmann is indicated by the fact that Jaspers and
Macquarrie arrive at almost contradictory interpretations of Bultmann's thought on this question. Jaspers argues that while Bultmann himself might not look upon persons outside the Christian
faith as "poor lost heathen," his thought leads inevitably in this
direction. According to Jaspers, any attempt to bind the decision
of faith to an objectively conceived divine proclamation results in
exclusivism.[65] Macquarrie, however, while admitting the ambiguity
in Bultmann's thought at this point, leads one to believe that he
does not really deny revelation outside the Christian faith.[66]

Professor Macquarrie admits that Bultmann occasionally speaks
as if there is no genuine knowledge of God or authentic existence
apart from the Christian kerygma. But, he says, Bultmann is
equivocal at this point, for he also maintains that "it is 'turning
from the world' which is the way to God, and that Christians and

64. *Ibid.*, p. 19.   65. *Myth*, pp. 78–79.
66. Macquarrie, *The Scope of Demythologizing*, pp. 173 ff.

non-Christians who have taken this step are unified in a 'community of the transcendent' which has nothing exclusive about it!"[67] Bultmann also says, "In every moment slumbers the possibility of being the eschatological moment. You must awaken to it."[68] Such passages suggest to Macquarrie that Bultmann is not really guilty of the type of exclusivism referred to by Jaspers.

Macquarrie's interpretation of Bultmann's view of the exclusiveness of revelation is indebted to the latter's understanding of revelation as an occurrence *in actu*, and on this basis he suggests that Bultmann's emphasis on the uniqueness of the Christian revelation expresses not its exclusive but its definitive character. The revelation *in actu* occurs within the historical tradition of the Christian faith. Insofar as revelation occurs here for me, it is said to have an ultimate or definitive character which necessarily excludes the validity of other truths for me. But this understanding of revelation is not, according to Macquarrie, incompatible with the recognition that there may be revelation for others which is not revelation for me.[69]

Schubert Odgen rejects Macquarrie's analysis at this point and repeats the charge of exclusivism made by Jaspers. In contrast to Macquarrie, Ogden finds Bultmann's thought quite unequivocal. Ogden maintains that the two passages cited by Macquarrie are taken out of context and hence misunderstood. He says that although Bultmann embraces atheists, nihilists, and believers in a community of the transcendent, he then asks whether we can speak of this community as having its existence in relation to God. And in answering this question, Bultmann is said to reaffirm his position claiming that authentic surrender to God comes only through faith in Jesus Christ. Thus the Christian community is distinguished from the world community in the transcendent. Further, according

67. *Ibid.*, p. 177; refers to *Essays*, pp. 301 ff.
68. *Ibid.*, p. 178; refers to Bultmann, *History and Eschatology* (New York: Harper and Row, 1957; Edinburgh: Edinburgh Univ. Press, 1957), p. 155.
69. *Ibid.*, pp. 179–182.

to Ogden, while Bultmann maintains that every moment contains
the possibility of being the eschatological moment, he understands
this possibility to be realized only in the Christian faith.[70]

Ogden's point of view is most clearly presented in his discussion
of authentic existence as possibility in principle and possibility in
fact. The contradiction in Bultmann's thought emerges, as he understands it, when Bultmann claims that Christian existence is a
possibility open to all men and then claims that it is a possibility
in fact only in the Christian faith. If, according to Ogden, Christian
existence is a possibility to all men, something for which they are
responsible, then either the distinction is vacuous or the possibility
in fact is not an original possibility for which man is responsible.[71]

Bultmann has in part defended himself against Ogden's criticism,
calling attention to Heidegger's distinction between an ontological
and an ontic possibility. Insofar as authentic existence is not *realized* in the philosophical (ontological) analysis of existence but is
chosen in personal existence, it is dependent on a decision in a
concrete historical situation. For Bultmann this concrete situation
occurs in the hearing of God's Word in the proclamation of the
Christian Church. Bultmann's most recent reply to Ogden is more
direct: "It would be false to deny that the 'possibility in principle'
—which I in fact do not contest—could become a 'possibility in
fact' without faith in Jesus Christ as a decisive act of God. God's
liberating act may occur everywhere, even if it is decisively revealed in the Word which Jesus speaks and which he is."[72]

Bultmann does, I believe, clarify one point that neither Jaspers
nor Ogden seems to appreciate fully. It is that a man who participates in a particular occurrence of revelation and chooses his authentic being in this context, implicitly at least denies the validity

    70. Ogden, *Christ without Myth*, pp. 174–175.
    71. *Ibid.*, pp. 117 ff.; see also pp. 71 ff.
    72. Bultmann, "Reply," p. 272. See Bultmann's review of Ogden's *Christ
without Myth* in *Journal of Religion*, XLII (July, 1962), 225–227, and John
Young Fenton, "The Post-Liberal Theology of Christ without Myth," *Journal
of Religion*, XLIII (April, 1963), 93–104.

of the claim that other revelations make upon him. Bultmann, for instance, says that it is meaningless to raise the question of absoluteness from within faith, "for then it has already been decided, since faith is the answer to revelation."[73] Bultmann is not writing comparative religion, and thus he is not seeking to discover the various relationships between the Christian religion and other religions which can be observed from outside the event of revelation. Rather he is seeking to communicate the occurrence that he has witnessed from within the community of faith. His primary concern is not to determine whether or not revelation occurs for others. His primary concern is to proclaim the revelation which has significance for his existence and the existence of the community in which he participates.

> Does Jaspers realize that wherever a revealed faith speaks, it asserts, and must assert, the absoluteness of its revelation, because it regards itself as the true fulfillment of the commandment: "I am the Lord thy God. . . . Thou shalt have no other gods before me.". . . At all events, it is absurd to look for various instances of revelation in the history of religion or the spirit. As a historian I can only discover various instances of faith in revelation, never of the revelation itself. For the revelation is revelation only *in actu* and only *pro me*; it is understood and recognized as such only in personal decision. . . . The Christian religion is a historical phenomenon, as other religions, and like the latter it can be considered with regard to its spiritual content and its existential understanding of man. Certainly the religions of this earth can be classified from the point of view of their spiritual content and the depth of their existential insight. But even if, in attempting such a classification, we were to give the Christian religion the highest rank. . . , this would mean something fundamentally different from the claim of the Christian faith to absoluteness. This

73. *Existence*, p. 89.

claim can—but also must—be raised by the believer only, not
on the basis of a comparison with other modes of faith, but
solely as answer to the word that is concretely addressed to
me.[74]

The problem is not that the Christian faith necessarily cancels
out other faiths but that the participant in the Christian revelation
understands himself and his relation to others on the basis of that
revelation, just as he understands love on the basis of his own act
of loving.

> Once again it is not that man is not subject to the demand to
> love his neighbour outside the realm of faith, nor that he could
> not know about it and fulfil the demand here and there, but
> that he who in faith is certain of the divine love, understands
> himself and his community with men simply on the basis of
> this love, and that it thus becomes the dominant and sustaining
> force of his life.[75]

It is, I believe, this view of revelation that Macquarrie has in
mind when he indicates Bultmann's view of revelation to be something other than exclusive. It is true, as Ogden says, that the community for Bultmann is fulfilled only in faith in the Christian revelation. But this is not so much a comparative judgment as a confession made from within the decision of faith. From the viewpoint
of faith, atheists, nihilists, and believers appear to be linked together in an inquiry which is fulfilled in the Christian faith.[76]

In spite of this, however, there are occasions when Bultmann
seems to step outside the limits imposed upon speech by an understanding of revelation *in actu* and make statements regarding other
claims to revelation which have the character of universally valid
statements. He says, for instance, that if man were to remain open
to the general revelation of God, God's Word would address him
in creation. Yet he follows this with the statement, "But, in fact,

74. *Myth*, pp. 67–71.   76. *Ibid.*
75. *Essays*, p. 303.

man just does not do this: he twists his negative knowledge into a positive knowledge, and so creation becomes mute for him who holds God's truth a prisoner."[77] In another place he suggests that Christian faith criticizes the answers of the non-Christian inquiry about God and not the inquiry itself. Christian faith asserts that "man apart from Christianity could not arrive at an answer at all, even if he carried on to the end in the clarity and seriousness of his inquiry. It asserts that *all answers* apart from the Christian answer are *illusions.*"[78]

Statements like these lend support to the criticism of exclusivism on the part of Bultmann and also to the criticism of ambiguity when seen in the light of his general point of view. Yet Bultmann never adequately clarifies the situation for us in spite of the fact that many persons have raised questions at this point. It is true that he makes clear the distinction between faith as a phenomenon in the history of the mind and faith as the answer to the question put to man in a particular revelation of God. He also indicates that the researcher of faith as a phenomenon of mind cannot judge whether or not a particular religion is based on revelation. He can only observe the inquiry about God and the various claims about revelation. It is reasonable for him to say that while there is continuity between Christian faith and other faiths at the level of inquiry, there is conflict at the point where different faiths make claims about the answer to the inquiry.[79] But this does not seem to provide the basis for his saying that "man apart from Christianity could not arrive at an answer at all, even if he carried on to the end in the clarity and seriousness of his inquiry" or that "*all answers* apart from the Christian answer are *illusions.*"[80] It is one thing to say that a particular claim to revelation has no meaning for me and another to say that it is illusory.

If Bultmann is to be consistent with his view of revelation *in actu*, he must repudiate statements of this type and make it more

77. *Ibid.*, pp. 114–115.   78. *Ibid.*, p. 98.
79. *Myth*, pp. 67 ff.; *Essays*, pp. 133 ff., 161.
80. *Essays*, p. 98.

obvious that the Christian faith's "rejection" of other faiths is actually an affirmation of the meaning of a particular event of revelation and not a rejection of the possibility that revelation be definitive or decisive for a person in another tradition. Bultmann is helpful in emphasizing the definitiveness of a revelatory event and in making clear that the particular affirmation of faith in Jesus Christ implicitly at least rejects claims to truth which would contradict it. It is this aspect of faith which is not given much scope by either Jaspers or Ogden. But this is no basis for the dismissal of other answers as illusions. Nor is it a basis for dismissing the possibility that revelation might be definitive for a person outside the Christian faith. Such an attitude not only makes impossible any genuine dialogue between religions but also falsifies the understanding of revelation as event.

Revelation and History

Jaspers admits that Bultmann struggles against the tendency to locate God unambiguously in an object in the world. Nevertheless, he concludes that Bultmann's thought leads inevitably in this direction when he asserts that God's encounter with man takes place by way of an event of the first century. The result, according to Jaspers, is that Bultmann retains the error of orthodoxy and objectifies the truth of revelation. In response to this criticism Bultmann maintains that Jaspers does not understand him adequately. He agrees that the "belief that 'God manifests himself at a given place and time, that he has revealed himself at one place and time and only there and then, makes God appear as a fixed thing, an object in the world.' "[81] And he is willing to admit that the Church often interprets revelation in this sense. But this is the very error which he has sought to correct.

If then, Jaspers and Bultmann are in essential agreement in their criticism of the objectification of revelation, where is the interpreter to look for that which distinguishes their thought and leads each to criticize the other? It is to be found, I believe, in their different approaches to the historicalness of truth. Generally speaking, Jaspers exemplifies what Kierkegaard has called the Socratic way to truth.[82] That is, the point of departure in time tends to be accidental, a vanishing moment, and the teacher can be no more than

81. *Myth*, p. 67.
82. Sören Kierkegaard, *Philosophical Fragments* (Princeton: Princeton Univ. Press, 1958), pp. 6 ff.

midwife. Ultimately each man is the center of truth. In contrast, Bultmann understands the moment in time to be of decisive significance. God reveals Himself in the event of Jesus as the Christ to man who is otherwise destitute of truth. The divine does for man what he cannot do for himself.

This is the point that Bultmann is trying to make when he accuses Jaspers of making Transcendence questionable and of failing to grasp the full significance of man's historicity. According to Bultmann, Jaspers believes that a "direct relation with the godhead is possible, for every man in his own responsible freedom of reason."[83] This is said to lead to a view like that of nineteenth-century Romanticism and Idealism in which Spirit is transcendent to physical presence but immanent to human reason. Bultmann admits that the Romantic conceived man to be inauthentic in himself and that he refused to equate empirical facts with revelation. Nevertheless, "man remains within himself; and he speculates about the identity of being and consciousness in order again to find himself even when he tries to get beyond himself."[84]

Jaspers seems dismayed when Bultmann goes so far as to relate his view of Transcendence with Schleiermacher's concept of the *Universum*. He attributes this to Bultmann's lack of acquaintance with his own work, particularly *Von der Wahrheit* and *Reason and Existenz*, saying simply, "I do not think it is possible to assert transcendence more resolutely than I have done in these works."[85] And there is a sense in which Jaspers' dismay is justified. For even if we argue that Schleiermacher underwent a development in his thought, there are still many passages in his works which could not be said to characterize Jaspers' idea of Transcendence.

It is true that for Jaspers Transcendence is said to have a power of attraction and that it stands in an immanent relation to the world, calling man to the One beyond the multiplicity of temporal

83. *Myth*, p. 66.
84. *Existence*, p. 68; see also *Myth*, pp. 66–67.
85. *Myth*, p. 97.

truths, and that reason is understood as an instrument of existence which opens it up to Transcendence. Yet it is not so much man's union with the transcendent that becomes apparent as his separation from it, his finiteness. Like Rudolf Otto, Jaspers seeks to combine the mystical and the theistic traditions with their ideas of union and separation. Reason does not flow from a primal source of being but, as the encompassing bond in continuous movement, encounters Transcendence in its unknowable rest. "The infinite which though unfathomable does enter into man's consciousness, causes man to transcend his finiteness by becoming aware of it."[86]

If, however, Jaspers can be defended against the extremes of nineteenth-century immanentism, the fact remains that his thought is similar and shares its more Socratic departure toward truth. That is, truth is something which is present to man if he will awaken to it. This is brought into focus when Bultmann accuses Jaspers of ignoring the summons and encounter in history. This means, says Bultmann, that Jaspers has not grasped the full significance of historicity, that historicity means for him only that "man is always situated at a certain point in time, that he lives under certain historical conditions, and is influenced by historical traditions."[87]

Jaspers apparently finds no serious problem with this characterization of his thought. He replies, "You reproach me for ignoring the earnestness of the summons, of the encounter. I will not contradict you on this point, all I can say is: The fact is, I know a Thou, I know a summons and encounter only among men."[88] Whereas Bultmann maintains that man chooses his authentic existence only in response to the divine encounter in the proclamation of the Church, Jaspers says, "what takes place is the awakening of the nobility in man created in God's image and likeness."[89]

This distinction is further clarified in Bultmann's Gifford Lectures, where he develops the idea of historicity as man's possibility

86. *Perennial Scope*, p. 64.
87. *Myth*, p. 66.
88. *Ibid.*, p. 97.
89. *Ibid.*, p. 74.

of being, suggesting that man participates in his authentic existence only by his own decision or resolution. Whereas Croce had understood history primarily in terms of man as reason, Bultmann understands it primarily in terms of man's responsibility over against the future. Thus reason takes second place to decision in the face of encounter.[90]

Bultmann admits that Jaspers is also striving to understand history in this sense and that he may be understood to have made an advance beyond Croce. But he does not believe that Jaspers has as yet been able to express clearly enough this view of history. The result is that when Jaspers seeks a standpoint beyond history he ends up losing history. According to Bultmann, man finds a standpoint beyond history only in response to the encounter and summons of God in the proclamation of the Church.[91]

Bultmann's position is elaborated in his discussion of the idea of history in the thought of Frederick Gogarten and Martin Heidegger, where he distinguishes Gogarten's view from Heidegger's, saying that Gogarten "immediately goes on to interpret 'decision' as decision in the face of the thou, whereas for Heidegger it is a decision for the possibility of my own existence."[92] Bultmann admits that decision for Heidegger is not without relation to others, and he also acknowledges that Gogarten understands man in deciding to lay hold on a possibility of his own existence. However, the manner in which they understand the thou differs. "For Gogarten, namely, it is the thou that first discloses the transitoriness of my existence and constrains me to decision, while for Heidegger the other is first authentically disclosed . . . by my knowing myself under the eyes of death as placed in decision."[93]

Bultmann accounts for this distinction between Gogarten and Heidegger on the basis of the distinction between the ontic and

90. Bultmann's conception of historicity, as Macquarrie has noted, depends upon the development of this idea by Heidegger in *Being and Time*, pp. 444 ff. See *Kerygma und Mythos*, VI/1, p. 21; *G.V.*, I, p. 118; and *History and Eschatology*, pp. 142 ff.
91. *History and Eschatology*, pp. 129 ff., 154.
92. *Existence*, p. 103.   93. *Ibid.*

ontological understanding of man. Decision is actually realized for Gogarten and Bultmann only where the I decides for the thou. And insofar as Heidegger makes an existential analysis and speaks about the ontological, he has neither the occasion nor the right to speak about the factual, the ontic experience. Theology does not contradict the ontological analysis. It does not even reject philosophy's ontic phenomenon of death as the striking phenomenon in which man's limitation is displayed. Rather, theology sees "on the one hand, that God encounters the natural man in death and, on the other hand, that the encounter with revelation means nothing more and nothing less than death for the natural man—that love is an absolute surrender of the I and only as such 'overcomes' death."[94] Theology does not reject the decision in the face of death. It does maintain that this decision is one of despair, that man is in fact choosing only what he already is, that man never frees himself from his past, and that this freedom, and consequently historicity as the possibility of an actual or new occurrence, arises only in faith's response to the proclamation of the Church. Here it is that the eternal thou is made understandable to man.[95]

Jaspers, of course, does not restrict decision in the manner that Heidegger does in *Being and Time*. Man, according to Jaspers, is authentically himself only as he chooses himself in relation to Transcendence. Thus freedom, historicity, and transcendent Being are interrelated for him as they are for Bultmann. For Jaspers, however, this relationship is not dependent upon an encounter with the thou in the proclamation of the Church but upon the pious soul's inner relation to Transcendence. "God does not speak through the commands and revelations of other men but in man's selfhood and through his freedom, not from without but from within."[96] Elsewhere, Jaspers writes:

> This reality [God] is accessible to existence through the orientation toward God that lies at its source. Hence faith in God,

94. *Ibid.*, pp. 109–110. 96. *Wisdom*, p. 90.
95. *Ibid.*, pp. 107–108.

springing as it does from the source, resists any mediation. This faith is not laid down in any definite articles of faith applicable to all men or in any historical reality which mediates between man and God and is the same for all men. The individual, always in his own historicity, stands rather in an immediate, independent relation to God that requires no intermediary.[97]

One cannot on the basis of statements like this simply dismiss Jaspers as a subjectivist. He escapes this in his suggestion that philosophical reflection which seeks to awaken our primal source is fulfilled only in communication with others. Without communication man is subject to error and is liable to the seduction of inauthentic self assertion. And without communication Transcendence would remain a void, its truth an unreality.[98] However, communication in the sense that Jaspers uses it cannot encounter us with a historical truth for which we must decide. It only provides the occasion for the inner awakening to selfhood. "Philosophy does not give, it can only awaken—it can remind, and help us to secure and preserve. In it each of us understands what he actually knew before."[99]

Thus Jaspers seems to return finally to the Socratic departure toward truth. That is, although he acknowledges our relation to tradition and to other persons in communication and even maintains that the truth of Transcendence emerges for us only in this context, he still makes the disclosure of truth an inner act in which we awaken to that which is already present to us. Here lies both the source of Bultmann's criticism of immanentism in Jaspers' thought and Jaspers' wilful separation from Bultmann. That Jaspers is willing to accept this characterization of his thought is demonstrated in the following passage:

> "The stumbling block" is an essential element of philosophical communication, too. But the term means radically different things according to whether it denotes stimulus to belief or

97. *Ibid.*, p. 47.   99. *Wisdom*, p. 51.
98. *Reason*, p. 79.

communication of belief. This distinction was formulated by Kierkegaard: Socrates is such a stimulus or gadfly; one man cannot give another the truth of faith, he can only make him aware of the truth that is hidden in him. But Christ, each time the Word is proclaimed, gives the faith itself along with the truth, that is, he gives the grace enabling us to believe what has been proclaimed.

You seem to mitigate the stumbling block of faith by distinguishing between the absoluteness of the Christian faith and the absoluteness of the Christian religion. I can understand this distinction only as implying that faith nevertheless justifies the practice of religion in history. . . . But, while the idea of an invisible church, a pure Biblical religion, or an absolute faith which becomes event only in the individual, is useful as a signpost, it becomes real only in visible churches, in historically determined denominations, in living individuals. That signpost may be the stumbling block, because it reminds us of what is really essential. But this essential must always be translated into reality in order to exist at all. This much, I think, I can understand. But if that signpost is to function as the stumbling block of the Christian faith, it is no longer a Socratic gadfly. And if that is your meaning when you describe your concept of demythologization as "a parallel to the Paulinian doctrine of justification by faith alone without the works of the law," I cannot follow you. . . . The truth of your faith claims exclusivity on the ground that it is based upon divine proclamation. The truth of philosophical faith is communicated by words and deeds, becoming in communication a stimulus to others to find themselves by following similar paths in their own historicity.[100]

The irony of this situation is that Jaspers' separation from Bultmann at this point is at the same time a separation from what he considers to be Bultmann's immanentism. Jaspers sees only two

100. *Myth*, pp. 79–80.

possible definitions of revelation. Either it is identified with an objective event in time or it is free from all particular events and occurs in the moment of individual existence when man awakens to the presence of the Eternal. Jaspers and Bultmann agree in rejecting the first, and Bultmann disagrees with Jaspers when he takes up the second. This means that Bultmann intends a third view of revelation, one, he maintains, that Jaspers never understands, one which to Jaspers is only a return to an identification of revelation with objective fixation.[101]

Bultmann is struggling to avoid the kind of immanentism of which Jaspers accuses him and considers himself able to do so on the basis of the paradox of the Christian faith which he believes has not yet been successfully communicated to Jaspers.[102] Bultmann does not offer an apology for this paradox but seeks rather to elucidate it as the offense of the Christian Gospel so that the decision of faith might be clairfied for the hearer.[103]

The Christian faith speaks of a historical (*historisch*) event which is at the same time the eschatological event, the event which sets an end to the world and its history. This paradox is presented in the New Testament in its witness to Jesus as the Messiah who in the fullness of time brings in the age of salvation and sets an end to the existing world. In him the old aeon has reached its end and the new begun.[104] This paradox, clothed in mythological language, was not always clear in primitive Christianity but was brought to clear expression by Paul and John. The man, Jesus of Nazareth, could in no way legitimize himself as the Word of God. He is legitimized only through the encounter with the Word itself, that is, only in the present moment of human existence when the objective historical event becomes the eschatological event. It is the offense of the Christian faith that an ordinary world event,

---

101. *Myth*, pp. 76 ff.; Bultmann, *Glauben und Verstehen*, III (Tübingen: J.C.B. Mohr [Paul Siebeck], 1962), 206 ff. Cited hereinafter as *G.V.*, III.
102. *Myth*, p. 71.
103. *G.V.*, III, p. 212.
104. *Ibid.*, p. 202.

which is no more than that to observation, becomes for faith the eschatological event, the event in which man is released from his past and is freed for God's future.[105]

This paradox of the Christian faith, according to Bultmann, is misunderstood if it is seen as an event of the past. If one looks to the past one seeks the skandalon of the Christian faith in something that is available to observation. However, the true skandalon is an event in which the selfhood of the believer is actually altered, put into a new relationship with God. It is not a logical contradiction but an existential event, an occurrence in the present in which one experiences freedom from one's old self and freedom for one's new self.[106]

But how does this paradox become a present reality for me? According to Bultmann it is present in the proclamation of the Church as we respond to it in faith or unbelief.[107] In the preaching God becomes present to me as my God, summoning me to decision before Him. In itself the sermon is only the word of man but it becomes the eschatological event of God in the moment when God's Word addresses me in the human word, when I am confronted with the decision to live out of my past or God's future. And this decision looks back to Jesus as evidence that the eschatological event has its origin in time, that it is not simply referring to a system of general truths.[108]

For Bultmann, the skandalon of the Christian faith is not something that he has decided upon arbitrarily. It is not an artificial limit to demythologizing. Rather, it is something that has addressed him in history and has demanded a decision from him. It is the point at which he begins demythologizing the New Testament, not the last vestige of mythology. Yet it is doubtful if Jaspers has clearly understood this paradoxical aspect of the Christian faith. At any rate, it is clear that he does not acknowledge the "stumbling block" which Bultmann has attempted to put before

105. *Ibid.*, pp. 202–205.
106. *Ibid.*, p. 205.
107. *Ibid.*, pp. 205–206.
108. *Myth*, p. 70.

him. For Jaspers the only significant skandalon is the "scandalous fact that Jesus, God's representative on earth, suffered the most disgraceful and painful death."[109] According to Jaspers, Bultmann overlooks this genuine stumbling block and proclaims a false one.

> The story of terrible injustice done to an innocent man, who was put to death like a criminal slave, with its emphasis on the reality of boundless suffering, has cast an illuminating light on the inevitability of all human suffering and on the human capacity for suffering, and it can help preserve us from Stoic apathy. It is *this* stumbling block—like the one inherent in the idea that man is given to himself—that, as I see it, can still be genuine today. We resist it and we respect it; and when this myth speaks to us, we see everything in a new light.[110]

The stumbling block Jaspers observes is not that of God's Word addressing man in human words but one in which the limits to human existence are indicated. Jaspers, consciously or unconsciously under the influence of the Christian faith, does not wish to detach the experience of Transcendence from history. He allows himself to be questioned by history, and in this way the myths and symbols speak to him. But the answer to these questions seems to come from beyond history. The illumination or awakening is mediated through nature and history but is finally fulfilled only in detachment from it. History thus is a scaffolding which can be removed as soon as the building is completed. Jaspers wants to retain the scaffolding because it is necessary to communication and makes God's revelation something different from that conceived by the mystic who soars up and away from history, but he believes that any real relation between history and revelation results in the latter's objectification and falsification. Jaspers stands very near to Bultmann but he does not accept the paradoxical unity of time and eternity which Bultmann finds in the proclamation of the Church. He hears in the kerygma only the word of man.

109. *Ibid.*, pp. 83–84.   110. *Ibid.*, p. 84.

Jaspers' view of revelation makes it difficult for him to appreciate the theologian's claim to a definitive revelation. He is aware that men are born into a particular historical tradition and develop in relation to it. He acknowledges his own debt to the biblical tradition and admits that man apart from the tradition would be nothing. Europeans, according to him, are what they are in virtue of the biblical religion and the secularizations which have their source in it. "It is a simple fact that without the Bible we pass into nothing. We cannot abandon our historical origin."[111] Yet he maintains the relativity and ambiguity of every tradition. Tradition, whether authoritarian or kerygmatic, seems to have no particular claim on man.

Jaspers' refusal to give any definitive status to tradition is no doubt motivated by his rejection of the exclusivism of revelation and his continual call to the existential sense of revelation. But he seems to overlook the fact that if all men followed his direction there would be no tradition. If we encounter truth from within a particular tradition, our confession of this truth inevitably involves the facts of this tradition. And this confession implicitly at least rejects other conflicting claims to truth. This is not to say, however, that confession leads necessarily to exclusivism. As Paul Tillich says, "the problem is not the right of rejecting that which rejects us; rather it is the nature of this rejection."[112]

When Christian faith speaks, it speaks out of a confrontation with the Word of God which it has heard in the proclamation of the Christian Church. It has no other starting point than this historic faith, and the task of theology is to bring this faith to expression. In this manner the event of the Christian revelation takes on a definitive status. It is in relation to this event that faith has heard the Word of God, and it is in relation to this event that faith has its meaning. However, just because this is a historic con-

111. Jaspers, *The European Spirit* (London: S.C.M. Press, 1948; New York: Macmillan, 1948), p. 60.
112. Paul Tillich, *Christianity and the Encounter of the World Religions* (New York: Columbia Univ. Press, 1963), p. 29.

fession it can never universalize itself so as to exclude all other claims to truth.

Bultmann indicates his appreciation for this historic confession when he refuses to take up the exclusive position of some earlier missionaries for whom all other religions were regarded as idolatrous. At least he does not reject the inquiries of persons outside the Christian faith but seeks to penetrate and illuminate them.[113] But when he concludes as he does at times that all answers to this inquiry are illusions, he seems to be denying the historical nature of revelation. If revelation is *in actu*, Christian faith must remain agnostic about the possibility of an answer's being found to man's inquiry outside the Christian revelation.[114] It certainly cannot say whether or not other persons have encountered a definitive revelation of God since revelation cannot be grasped except from within the revelatory moment itself.

It is true that other claims to revelation may be understood by us only from the point of view of that revelation which is definitive for us. Nevertheless, if we maintain that revelation is only *in actu* and if we acknowledge the limits of our finite perspective, it seems that we must maintain the possibility that God might address other persons definitively in ways that differ from the way in which we have heard His address. Indeed, some such approach might be necessary in order to explain the variety of expressions of revelation from within the Christian Church itself.

The revelation of God in Jesus Christ is a definitive occurrence which illuminates other events and enables the believer to understand them. In this light, the believer is able to recognize the activity of God in man's inquiry about Him and to criticize the various answers to this inquiry. This, however, does not mean that revelation cannot occur for others in historical situations. The only

113. *Essays*, p. 98.
114. John Young Fenton, "The Post-Liberal Theology," p. 99, and John Macquarrie, *The Scope of Demythologizing*, pp. 183 ff. reach similar conclusions. The clearest statement of Macquarrie's position is found in his *Principles of Christian Theology* (London: S.C.M. Press, 1967, and New York: Scribner's, 1966), pp. 134–158.

way that I could deny a definitive revelation to other persons would be from within their particular history, and this may not in fact be a live option for me. Thus the relationship between revelation in one history and in another is neither an either/or nor a unity of both, but a dialectic in which the confession arising out of one event is challenged by the confession of another and vice versa. We may never get beyond the dialectic in any final way, and yet we may, in the midst of the dialectic, become more deeply aware of the meaning of revelation.

This approach to the problem of exclusivism in religion has much in common with Jaspers' point of view. Yet it differs at two important points. First, Jaspers assumes that the other person's claim to truth is valid. This seems, however, to necessitate my being able to stand outside history and observe it, which is not a real possibility, if, as both Jaspers and Bultmann have said, revelation is an occurrence from within history. Second, Jaspers' demand that history be interpreted as a cipher seems to mean that I must transcend the very history within which revelation has occurred for me. The result is the elimination of the historical or at least the reduction of it to a subjective moment in experience, and revelation is left without any real meaning. If revelation is to have any significance it would seem that it must jealously guard its being as a historical event.

III Faith and Language

Theory of Language

Jaspers' philosophy, as we have said, may be characterized as a philosophizing of the Encompassing, a way of thinking toward that which is neither subject nor object but which is disclosed in the subject-object dichotomy. The Encompassing, understood as Transcendence, becomes other than a void only in the historical moment of Existenz, and this is affirmed in philosophical faith. It follows that faith is neither subjective nor objective but refers to that which is other than subject or object and yet is inseparable from them.

The problem that this poses for language and communication is far-reaching. Philosophical faith seeks to communicate Transcendence as it is understood in Existenz. Yet the language of neither subject nor object is adequate to this task. Objective statements have reference to universally valid ideas and cannot refer to that which is not comprehended within these limits. Yet subjective or emotive statements cannot refer beyond themselves, cannot refer to something beyond the subject side of the subject-object dichotomy. Jaspers' problem then is one of speaking of that which Existenz understands but is unable to objectify without losing.

The language which Jaspers proposes for this task is that of the cipher. Transcendence manifests itself in the subject-object dichotomy. But its objectivity is neither the tangible object nor the rational idea. It is the myth or symbol understood as cipher. The term cipher has its origin in the act of replacing the written characters of language with ciphers, code symbols which require interpretation in order to be understood. This basic idea has been expanded in philosophical thought in speaking of the *Weltgeist*,

which requires to be interpreted by man. Being, hidden in the
script of the world, is known through a proper deciphering or
reading of the script.[1] Cipher, as Jaspers understands it, is not
something that can be equated with universally valid knowledge.
It is rather that which lights up in the ground of things. It withdraws from all universally valid experience and verifiability. Its
truth lies in its interrelationship with human existence.[2]

First, then, cipher is not to be equated with any particular objective form. Properly understood, it is objectivity in suspension. The
cipher is understood as the speech of Transcendence, which takes
place not simply in a world out there but in the midst of my relating myself as a subject to an object. Both the subjective and objective structures of reality are essential to the cipher's becoming the
speech of Transcendence. That is, there is no direct speech which
bypasses the world, and any object within the world, including
thought itself, and the foundering of human existence at its limits,
is a potential cipher. But, in every situation the object must be
transformed in such a way that it becomes transparent to the
hidden speech of Transcendence.

Because the cipher does not come to appearance directly but
only from within the world, Jaspers speaks at times of an outer
knowing of the cipher. Thus he says that we know ciphers in
collecting and arranging myths, symbols, and so on, that is, in the
historical study of these forms. But this outer knowing becomes
inner knowing when we become concerned with them in our
Existenz. And it is only in the inner knowing that the depth of the
myth is disclosed.[3] It is this which permits Jaspers to support the
validity of myth over against what he considers to be the destruc-
tion of myth in Bultmann's program of demythologizing. Jaspers
is sympathetic with demythologizing insofar as it reacts against
what he considers to be the falsification of myth when literal and

1. The history of the cipher is outlined in *Wörterbuch der philosophischen Begriffe*, ed. J. Von Hoffmeister (Hamburg: Felix Meiner, 1955), p. 139.
2. *Offenbarung*, pp. 153 ff.
3. *Ibid.*, pp. 154–155.

material reality is ascribed to its symbols. But he believes that myth understood "historically" is essential to the communication of Transcendence. He would interpret myths so that the transcendent Reality might be disclosed to Existenz.[4]

> When I speak of de-mythification, I do not mean the translation of mythical content into something like a purer truth nor its interpretation in terms of some unmythical truth-content. I mean rather a passing beyond all myths,—the picturesque foregrounds of the infinite manifold,—to an unpictured godhead, which appears neither as a picture to the eye nor as thought to thinking, but which is the reality beyond all myths and beyond all possibilities of thinking, a reality, which is experienced and touched by us only in myths and thoughts.[5]

According to Jaspers there is no object or event which might not be understood as a cipher. Yet there is apparently nothing within the object itself which relates to its being a cipher. That is, while Jaspers indicates the importance of objectivity in man's experience of Transcendence, it is in the final analysis suspended. The cipher is the transformed object which hangs suspended between the two poles of the subject-object dichotomy. Perceptible objectivity (*Gegenständlichkeit*) is transformed into what Jaspers calls being an object (*Objectivität*). The perceptible object is said to be not destroyed but transformed into a cipher.[6]

In this state of suspended objectivity, the visible object becomes transparent to reality. This is elucidated in Jaspers' distinction between *deutbar* and *schaubar* symbolism. *Deutbar* symbolism refers to something final and definite such as the libido in psychoanalysis or the dialectic in the thought of Hegel. There is a determined *signatum* to which it refers. Symbol understood in this sense differs from cipher. In *schaubar* symbolism, however, the symbol is approached only from the depths of Existenz. It is an

---

4. *Myth*, p. 18; *Offenbarung*, p. 172.
5. Jaspers, "Reply to My Critics," pp. 782–783.
6. *Truth*, pp. 19, 38–39.

appearance which opens itself up in the present moment of my Existenz.[7] This understanding of symbol can be transferred to the cipher. Yet neither symbol nor cipher understood in this sense refers to anything fixed or objective. They refer to the transparency of objectivity in the relation of Transcendence to Existenz.

When the symbol becomes a cipher, I grasp reality in it. But when it is merely an object with a fixed meaning, essential reality is lost. In this state the symbol is said to collapse into a sign, a signification, or a metaphor. These fallen symbols may be arranged according to multiple points of view and may be understood to make up the world of potential ciphers. But they are said to have the same relation to their origin that bones have to a dead body. Once one begins to talk about symbols in a detached way, the symbols die. It is only when one proceeds from the symbol within the symbol that one reaches essential reality. Detached talk about the symbol may be understood as preparation for the reading of the symbol as cipher, but can never be equated with the cipher itself.[8]

In understanding the cipher as suspended and transparent objectivity, Jaspers draws our attention to the darkness at the borders of sensuous data, a darkness or a depth which cannot be penetrated at the level of objective knowledge. Philosophizing seeks to penetrate this depth. Jaspers claims that the sensuous is not abandoned in this act. But he also says, "Transparency of sensuousness signifies at the same time disassociation from sensuousness as such."[9] It is apparent that he wants to free Transcendence from all objective limitations, and yet he wants to do so without abandoning objectivity altogether.

Jaspers contrasts the appearance of Being in the transparency of the objective order with what he thinks to be the religious understanding of God's presence in the world. Religious corporeality is superior to pure bondage to transparentless realities insofar as

7. *Philosophie*, pp. 801–802.   9. *Ibid.*, p. 44.
8. *Truth*, p. 49.

it leads to an upswing to the supersensuous. But, in comparison to the presence of Being in philosophizing it appears as a distinctive empirical reality. Its end result is not the transparency of the sensuous but Transcendence bound to an empirical reality of the world.[10]

Second, the cipher is understood as the historical (*geschichtlich*) speech of Transcendence, a speech which can be known only in relation to Existenz. The cipher is not something present which signifies something absent, a here signifying a beyond. The signification of the cipher lies in a presentness which is not translatable into a knowledge of something. Thus, even as we speak of the cipher as the speech of Transcendence, we speak only metaphorically; its specific character as speech is never defined but only circumscribed.[11]

Transcendence is not, according to Jaspers, a void which is as if it were not. Yet because it is transcendent, it cannot become present in the immanent world as it is in itself. That is, Transcendence cannot become an object of knowledge. It is an immanent Transcendence of which Jaspers speaks, and he believes the cipher to be the vehicle of its communication. Ciphers are the spiritual realities in our speech but never the tangible presence of Transcendence itself. When the truth of Transcendence is thought to be contained in perceivable reality, Transcendence is lost.[12] Ciphers bring Transcendence to appearance not as tangible reality but as present reality for my Existenz.[13]

The speech of Transcendence in the cipher is immediate (*unmittelbar*) speech. It is that which is heard historically in the presentness of Existenz.[14] Ciphers bring Transcendence into the present through no knowledge or insight but alone in the illuminating power in the historicity of the individual. Thus the truth of Transcendence is a present existential truth, not a dead thing of the

10. *Ibid.*, p. 46.
11. *Ibid.*, pp. 41–42.
12. *Offenbarung*, p. 163.

13. *Philosophie*, pp. 792 ff.
14. *Ibid.*, pp. 786–788.

past. The cipher is being heard and appropriated as the speech of Transcendence when Existenz hears it and chooses to fulfill itself.[15]

The cipher then can be properly understood only in relation to Existenz. When Existenz hears the speech of Transcendence and comes to its true self, in that moment, we can speak properly of the cipher as the speech of Transcendence. This speech is not experienced in a definite concept but in Existenz reaching through to the bottomlessness of the object to the source of its meaning, which can be known only as present experience. The cipher is present as the speech of Transcendence in the moment of individual Existenz.[16]

Third, the signification of the cipher cannot be separated from that which is signified in it. The signification of the cipher is not that something present signifies something absent, but lies "in a presentness which is no longer translatable into knowledge of something."[17] The cipher is the presentness of Being which cannot be cognized but only listened to.[18] We are able to question the cipher as to its meaning, and in this questioning we may experience a deepening of the cipher. But in this inquiry we also become aware that no interpretation is sufficient. "The cipher is the inexhaustible signification with which no definite interpretation is commensurate, but which rather demands in the interpretation itself an endless movement of interpreting."[19] This interpretation is a metaphorical act, a game, not a form of cognition. That is, interpretation is a preparation to the manifestation of Being, but it can never interpret Being itself, which is the real presentness in the cipher. Being itself is nameless. "If we speak of it, then we use an infinite number of names and cancel them all again."[20]

The cipher then has no definite content, for its real content is not something which it signifies but the presentness of Being, which is in no way available as a content of knowledge. It is this

---

15. *Offenbarung*, pp. 172–185.
16. *Offenbarung*, pp. 173–174.
17. *Truth*, p. 42.

18. *Ibid.*, p. 41.
19. *Ibid.*, p. 42.
20. *Ibid.*

which leads Jaspers to distinguish among sign (*Zeichen*), symbol (*Symbol*), and cipher (*Chiffer*).[21] The sign indicates an other, but that other is present without the sign. Thus there is no necessary connection between the sign and that which it represents. As Paul Tillich would say, the sign does not participate in the reality to which it points.[22] The symbol is the presence of an other in which the symbol and the symbolized are inseparable. Because of this Jaspers at times uses symbol and cipher interchangeably. But he prefers to distinguish the cipher from the symbol because the former has the sense of a representation of an other whereas the cipher has the sense of speech, speech of a reality which can be spoken and thus only heard.

Finally, the cipher has the character of ambiguity. Jaspers' attack on the once-happenedness of revelation does not result from a view that there are many truths. He is not a relativist in allowing a number of truths, nor does he seek to gather the truth of all religions into one composite truth. He cannot be a relativist in either of these senses because truth cannot be contained in a knowable object in time. The one truth is historical, absolute in the existential moment of the individual. It is the unconditional truth for Existenz and just for this reason is not capable of finite interpretation or explanation.[23]

Jaspers will not permit this one truth to be bound to any particular object or tradition just because it is unconditional. The one truth may become apparent to Existenz in the depths of a variety of objects as they assume cipher status for me. But truth still stands beyond all the various truths contained in finite categories. These many truths are properly understood neither in excluding the variety in favor of one finite representation of truth (Christian orthodoxy, for instance) nor in remaining indifferent to other claims to truth. Rather, what is understood to be unrelated in the

21. *Offenbarung*, pp. 157–158; *Wahrheit*, pp. 256–257.
22. Paul Tillich, *Theology of Culture* (New York: Oxford Univ. Press, 1959), p. 54.
23. *Reason*, p. 100.

multiplicity of finite truths is thought by Jaspers to be related in Transcendence in the moment when man seeks the distant truth beyond all particular truths.[24]

Because of this the cipher always retains a sense of ambiguity. There can be no truth which is final and absolutely valid, for truth is existential. The unequivocalness of the cipher lies in Transcendence's being immediately present to me. Its equivocalness lies in Transcendence's approaching finite existence in time where it can never become universally valid.[25]

The language of the cipher, as Jaspers presents it, has a logical structure similar to that of traditional negative theologies. That is, the cipher does not really say anything about Transcendence; by leading us negatively through the world of objectivity it seeks to evoke a situation in which Transcendence may be discerned in Existenz. Jaspers agrees with Kierkegaard that faith is not an immediate experience which can be described as given but "a primal awareness of being through the mediation of history and thought."[26] It is an awareness that occurs not as man bypasses the world but as he transcends through the objectivity of the world. Otherwise Transcendence would remain a void.

> If it is asserted that, in this kind of philosophizing God turns into nothing, it is to be replied: this objection is valid only if the mode of knowing by consciousness-as-such (the intellect) is taken as the only and universally valid form in which reality is present. Philosophizing stands opposed to this: true, for it consciousness-as-such is the medium of all thinking, even of the transcending and speculative kind. But in this medium the appropriate and proper implementation occurs by way of the knowable reality of the being of the world. Making use of its forms, this medium is being surpassed wherever transcendent reality becomes present. The way this happens is that the objective, because of (inherent) contradictions, circles, and tautol-

---

24. *Ibid.*   26. *Perennial Scope*, p. 10.
25. *Philosophie*, pp. 796 ff.

ogies, becomes void as itself and thereby becomes the spring-board from which the leap takes place.[27]

It is this which permits Jaspers to say with the logical positivists that Transcendence is beyond the limits of perception and thought, while saying at the same time that what is unthinkable in the case of Transcendence is nevertheless real and capable of being communicated indirectly through cipher thinking, in which the objectivity of the world and thought becomes transparent to Transcendence.[28] However, insofar as the features of objective speech are put into suspension in the cipher, it is doubtful whether anything is in the final analysis said about transcendent Being. The leap Jaspers proposes beyond the limits of objectivity seems to be a leap into silence. It appears that nothing of significance may be said about Transcendence.

Bultmann is also concerned with the objectification of the transcendent in myths and symbols. He calls for a program of demythologizing or existential interpretation which invites comparison with Jaspers' reading of the cipher script. Demythologizing as Bultmann understands it is a method of interpretation whereby the essential meaning or intention of myth is disclosed. Its real purpose is not one of eliminating the myths of the Bible but of interpreting them so that the Bible and the Church's teaching may be heard as a summons. Bultmann presents this problem to Jaspers as one of teaching and preaching concerning texts dealing with the resurrection of Jesus in the flesh, demons, and so on. The problem is greater than that of calling attention to mythical language itself. It is one of actually supplying a method to interpret biblical texts and to guide pastors in the development of their sermons.[29]

Bultmann's program of demythologizing, as is well known, has come under the scrutiny and criticism of many scholars and is a specialized study in itself which we are not able to follow here in any detail. However, it is necessary that we consider it insofar as

27. Jaspers, "Reply to My Critics," p. 783.
28. *Reason*, p. 105.   29. *Myth*, pp. 60 ff.

it is of importance to Bultmann's theory of religious language.

There is little doubt that some of the criticisms of Bultmann's program could have been avoided had he been more cautious in his early attempts to present formal definitions of myth and mythology. In his programmatic essay, for instance, he defined mythology as "the use of imagery to express the otherworldly in terms of this world and the divine in terms of human life, the other side in terms of this side."[30] As a formal definition this says, as Ronald Hepburn observes, that any language used to refer to or represent the divine is mythological.[31] Yet, in this same essay, Bultmann draws a distinction between the type of mythology that he would eliminate and mythology in a broader sense in which any language about an act of God is mythological. And in a later essay he suggests that the language appropriate to speaking of an act of God is not mythological but analogical.[32]

In spite of the confusion suggested here, however, Bultmann does operate within a general scheme that the interpreter is able to follow. This scheme or point of view is suggested in an essay entitled "What Sense Is There to Speak of God?" where he makes the distinction between speaking about God (*über Gott*) and speaking of or out of God (*von Gott* or *aus Gott*). To speak about God is to make God into an object, to assume a neutral standpoint outside God and hence to lose Him. According to Bultmann there can be no universal truths about God which have validity apart from the concrete situation in which God addresses the speaker. Indeed it is not only an error to speak about God in the fashion of a science, it is also sin insofar as it becomes an undertaking of the speaker and is dependent on him.[33]

30. *Kerygma and Myth* (London, 1957), p. 10, n. 2.
31. Ronald Hepburn, "Demythologizing and the Problem of Validity," in *New Essays in Philosophical Theology*, ed. A. Flew and A. MacIntyre (London: S.C.M. Press, 1958, and New York: Macmillan, 1964), pp. 229 ff. John Macquarrie has adequately defended his claim that Bultmann's definition of myth is ambiguous against Schubert Ogden's claim to the contrary. See Macquarrie, *Studies in Christian Existentialism* (London: S.C.M. Press, 1966), pp. 160 ff., and Ogden, *Christ without Myth*, pp. 28–31, 166–169.
32. *Kerygma and Myth* (London, 1957), pp. 43, 197.
33. *G.V.*, I, pp. 26–33.

Demythologizing may be understood as a critique of all attempts to say anything *about* God. When one thinks mythologically one forgets the essential intention of myth "to speak of the existence of men in their being grounded and limited through a transcendent and unworldly power, a power which is not perceivable in objectifying thought."[34] Instead one objectifies the transcendent and makes it into an object which is at the disposal of man, capable of being controlled and influenced by him. Mythological thinking in this sense contradicts the Kantian tradition in philosophy and also the Protestant view of faith which is unable to secure itself in the subject-object dichotomy. Thus, the first task of demythologizing is one of criticizing all attempts to identify immanent realities with the transcendent. It is a negative task insofar as mythical thinking is said to conceal the essential intention of myth.

This critique of mythology, however, does not result in the elimination of all myths. On the contrary, it points up the symbolic sense of myth. "Mythological conceptions can be used as symbols or images which are perhaps necessary to the language of religion and therefore also of the Christian faith."[35] In this case myth loses its mythological or objectifying sense. It has become what Tillich calls a "broken myth," one whose mythological sense is acknowledged and one which cannot be replaced by scientific substitutes.[36] This view of myth coincides with Jaspers' view of the myth as cipher, a comparison which Bultmann invites when he asks:

> Disregarding the question of whether this reality can be expressed only in mythological language, as Jaspers maintains, I should like to ask whether his conception of myth, in so far as he defines it as a statement in cipher, is so different from my own. When I say that the myth expresses man's knowledge of the grounds and limits of his being, is this so different from

---

34. *Kerygma und Mythos*, II, p. 184; and *Kerygma und Mythos*, VI/1, pp. 23 ff.

35. *Mythology*, p. 67.

36. Paul Tillich, *Dynamics of Faith* (New York: Harper and Row, 1958), pp. 50–51. John Macquarrie has made this connection between demythologizing and "broken myth" in *The Scope of Demythologizing*, pp. 203 ff.

what Jaspers implies? At all events, I agree with him that myth is misunderstood when the reality it denotes is conceived of as empirical, and its language as that of "a guaranteed and guaranteeing physical presence."[37]

Just as Jaspers' critique of the objectification of the transcendent in immanent categories does not eliminate all oblique references to the otherworldly, so Bultmann does not intend to eliminate all such references. If mythology is eliminated in the narrow sense of identifying the transcendent with the immanent, it is not eliminated in the sense that one regards all language about an act of God as mythological. There are in fact, says Bultmann, terms such as Transcendence which in the broader sense are fundamentally mythological.[38] Such terms, however, cannot speak about God in the sense of assigning a definite content to him any more than they can for Jaspers. Since God can be known only in the concrete moment of personal existence, any positive description of Him which has the character of general propositions misses Him. They transpose Him into this world and lose Him.[39]

To this point then, there is little difference between Bultmann's and Jaspers' theory of the language of faith. Beyond this point, however, a clear distinction at least in intention makes its appearance. Jaspers' openness to all myths results in the emptying of myths of any specific understanding. Although he urges through communication a struggle between myths, all myths are finally understood as ciphers in a way that makes unimportant the different interpretations of the self's relation to Transcendence which are reflected in the variety of myths available to us. In contrast to this, Bultmann undertakes to translate the particular understanding of the self in the biblical myths in order that the hearer may understand it as a summons.

Jaspers has never understood this hermeneutical task, according to Bultmann; the cipher does no more than describe the problem

37. *Myth*, p. 61, n. 1.
38. *Kerygma and Myth* (London, 1957), pp. 43–44, 103.
39. *Mythology*, p. 66.

of interpretation. All myths refer to a reality beyond the empirical. But the question is whether this reality and hence human existence are understood alike in all mythologies. The real hermeneutic task as it confronts Bultmann is that of interpreting the Bible and the teachings of the Church so that they may be heard as an address. But how would Jaspers do this, asks Bultmann. He says that the redemptive history "must be tested existentially and judged on the basis of the strength that emanates from its language, and the truth that arises from it in the reality of life." But the question is, "How is this done?"[40]

Bultmann's reply to his own question is that the self-understanding of the New Testament may be translated and hence clarified in the existentialist language of Martin Heidegger. This is possible because the philosopher is saying the same thing about human existence as the New Testament and saying it independently. By clarifying the New Testament understanding of human existence in this manner, Bultmann is witnessing to the fact that faith is more than a mere *sacrificium intellectus*, that it actually involves a decision between two ways of understanding oneself, as bound to the world or free from it.

This is not to say, however, that the language of philosophical analysis is appropriate to speech about God. As John Young Fenton says, "If existentialist language is used to talk about God it also must be demythologized, because God is not 'there' (*vorhanden*), available for existentialist analysis."[41] Philosophical analysis might discuss the *concept* of God, a discussion in which believers and non-believers might participate. But it cannot speak of God, who is known only in the moment of personal existence. Thus, although Heidegger's distinction between existential and existentiell understanding permits Bultmann to speak in a definite way of human existence without losing its personal or concrete sense, it does not permit him to speak of God.

This means that if Bultmann is to complete his task of interpre-

---

40. *Myth*, p. 61.
41. Fenton, "The Post-Liberal Theology," p. 97.

tation he requires a language appropriate to faith's speaking of
God. This is indicated when he asks if the conception of Transcendence, which remains after the myths have been broken, is an
exclusively negative concept. In other words, is any language of an
act of God possible, or are we put into the position of having to
leave Him in the realm of the unspeakable? This would be the
case, according to Bultmann, only if to speak of God did not mean
to speak at the same time of our personal existence.

> If God's action must be thought of as hidden, how is it possible
> to speak of it except in purely negative statements? Is the con-
> ception of transcendence an exclusively negative conception? It
> would be if to speak of God did not also mean to speak of
> our personal existence. If we speak of God as acting in general,
> transcendence would indeed be a purely negative conception,
> since every positive description of transcendence transposes it
> into this world. It is wrong to speak of God as acting in
> general statements, in terms of the formal analysis of human
> existence. It is precisely the formal, existentialist analysis of
> human existence which shows that it is indeed impossible to
> speak of our personal existence in general statements. I can
> speak of my personal existence only here and now in the con-
> crete situation of my life. To be sure, I can explicate in general
> statements the meaning, the sense of the conception of God
> and God's action in so far as I can say that God is the power
> which bestows upon me life and existence, and in so far as I
> can describe these actions as the encounter which demands my
> own personal decision. By doing so I acknowledge that I can-
> not speak of God's action in general statements; I can speak
> only of what He does here and now with me, of what He speaks
> here and now to me.[42]

The sum of this divergence between Jaspers and Bultmann is
that the latter, at the precise point where myth loses its significance

42. *Mythology*, p. 66.

and Transcendence becomes a negative conception, introduces a dimension of language other than that of existential analysis. This is the language of analogy. Analogy first makes its appearance in Bultmann's work in his reply to critics who suggest that de-mythologizing either would make it impossible to speak of an act of God or would reduce it to the description of a subjective experience. To this Bultmann replies that an act of God must denote an act in a real and "objective" sense, that it must be more than a subjective creation of man. Yet this act cannot be conceived in the objectivity of a worldly phenomenon capable of being observed or in the objectivity of philosophical analysis. Rather, since God is for me only here and now, I can speak of Him only by simultaneously speaking of myself as the one who is existentially concerned. Such speech would be analogical in that it "assumes an analogy between the activity of God and that of man and between the fellowship of God and man and that of man with man."[43]

Bultmann is obviously aware of the problems of negativism in religious language and may be understood to be seeking a way beyond the limits of a thoroughgoing existentialism. He senses a need for a more definite language of God and yet is restricted by the awareness that a neutral statement cannot speak of God as He is for me in my concrete existence. Analogy is proposed as the solution to this problem. Yet when we are confronted with an example of this type of language we seem to be a long way from any solution to our problem. For instance, we read that when we speak of God's love and care we are using analogies and that "these conceptions mean real experiences of God as acting here and now."[44] Or again we read that the affirmation that God is creator "can only be a personal confession that I understand myself to be a creature which owes its existence to God."[45] In spite of his desire to make God other than a negative with regard to thought, he seems to leave Him in that realm. We speak of our

---

43. *Kerygma and Myth* (London, 1957), p. 197.
44. *Mythology*, p. 69.   45. *Ibid.*

experiences or our understanding of ourselves, but we seem to be unable to say anything about that which makes our experience other than merely emotive.

Perhaps most will agree that Bultmann is making a valid point. There is a distinction between loving and a psychological account of love, and there is a distinction between God's acting toward me as love and a neutral philosophical inquiry about the idea of God as love. But there is also, it would seem, a dimension in which, through reflection, I bring to expression the concrete event in which love occurs. Here I seek to understand not simply how I feel but also the object toward which my feelings are directed. To say that God loves me or cares for me or that I am his creature is surely to say something with reference to God. Otherwise there may be no basis for my experience or feeling. William Hordern makes this point in noting that when the writer of John says that God is love, "we can ask whether this statement is objectively true or only an expression of John's feeling.[46] Bultmann's restriction on language of God would seem to say that we can never really get beyond the language of personal prayer.

It is this attitude toward religious language which has brought him into conflict with those who are sympathetic with his point of view and yet seek to supplement it with a more definite ontology. They too wish to avoid making a neutral philosophical statement about God but in their different ways declare that we may speak of God in the context of reality as a whole without turning Him into a neutral object. Heinrich Ott, for instance, suggests, on the basis of his studies of the so-called later Heidegger, that theology may speak of God without His becoming a neuter category. But Bultmann replies that theology does not in fact have this character, that lectures on theology "are not a witness in which the theologian presents himself as a believer, but are more nearly an 'unbelieving'

46. William Hordern, *Speaking of God* (New York: Macmillan, 1964), p. 157.

thought-process of an objectifying kind."[47] For similar reasons Bultmann resists the proposal of Macquarrie that his thought be supplemented by a more definite ontological setting and the proposal of Schubert Ogden that analogy may be used to speak not only indirectly of God in terms of human existence but also of God and God's action without God being turned into an object.[48]

Bultmann reminds us on several occasions, of course, that his task is the hermeneutical one. We also need to keep in mind that unless faith is assent to doctrine it is the Word of God which must be communicated. And this Word, as Ebeling reminds us, is a historical event which involves a relation between persons. The preacher is seeking to bring the hearer into a relation with this Word, to communicate participation rather than propositions.[49] But if his language is to mediate a relation between man and God, then surely his language must be capable of referring beyond the subject's side of experience. If Bultmann is to be consistent in his attempt to speak of the encounter of existence with God, it would seem that he would find himself pushed more and more toward a clarification of the meaning of God and a presentation of a language which is adequate to express God as He is meaningful for human existence.

Unless this task is undertaken, the language which attempts to speak of God as He is for us will tend either to reduce God to a void (in which case there is no advance upon Jaspers) or to take on the appearance of an arbitrary and authoritative statement which is unable to make any claim to truth. Faith may be unable to prove itself at the level of universally valid knowledge. But to

---

47. From a letter to Heinrich Ott on his publication of *Denken und Sein*, as summarized by James Robinson in the volume edited by Robinson and John Cobb, Jr., *The Later Heidegger and Theology* (New York: Harper and Row, 1963), p. 48.

48. Bultmann, "Reply," pp. 271 ff.

49. Gerhard Ebeling, *Word and Faith* (London: S.C.M. Press, 1963), pp. 326–327.

say that its object is outside the realm of reflection and that "faith, speaking of God as acting, cannot defend itself against the charge of illusion" is to admit that God has no real meaning in the context of the world.[50] Philosophy may play a role in suggesting that faith is at least a possibility. But it is the task of theology to indicate how faith's decision makes sense in view of this possibility. The language of theology would not be the neutral statement of a philosopher, however, but the confessional statement of a believer.

50. *Mythology*, p. 71.

Language and Communication

Man's encounter with Transcendence is, according to Jaspers, historical in the sense that it is "the existential possibility of achieving and experiencing the actual unity of time and eternity in the moment" which is "grasped out of existential freedom."[51] In other words it is for man a unique occurrence, an individual truth which transforms the one who encounters it and yet cannot be spoken of in universally valid terms because it is historical in this sense. It follows that communication cannot be direct in the sense of pouring truth from one vessel into another, for the uniqueness and individuality of the event would be lost. According to Jaspers, a form of indirect communication is called for in which an individual's authentic existence may be illuminated by his struggle with others to understand himself and the world in which he is immersed.

Basic to this understanding of communication is Jaspers' understanding of man as bound up with other men. I am "I" only in relation to another. I grasp myself not as an isolated being but as one who is reciprocally related to another. And the fulfilment of my authentic existence comes about as I stand over against the other without rejecting his "I" in which my being is mirrored. This is not of course to suggest that I lose myself to the other. On the contrary, as in Hegel's discussion of the master-slave relationship, while I cannot cancel the other without losing myself, I encounter the other as a resistance over against which I must assert myself. Thus the awareness of myself is immersed in this reciprocity in

51. *Myth*, p. 99.

which I become myself through the other as he is through me. To remove ourselves from this reciprocity, to isolate ourselves, is to disappear into the nothingness of no content and to lose our authentic selfhood. This possibility is indicated in the past when deaf mutes who were deaf at birth remained undeveloped.[52]

If, then, man grasps himself only in the midst of a reciprocal relationship with others, the transcendent also makes its appearance in this context. It is this which permits Fritz Kaufmann to draw a distinction between Jaspers' philosophy and the teaching of Sankara and the Bhagavadgītā. If Jaspers' way of reality's being transfigured in the appearance of Transcendence is reminiscent of Hinduism, it differs in retaining the plurality of selves as opposed to the oneness of Atman.[53] The fulfilment of Existenz in relation to Transcendence is reason's final goal, but it is one attained only through communication between persons. "The certainty of authentic being resides only in unreserved communication between men who live together and vie with one another in a free community, who regard their association with one another as but a preliminary stage, who take nothing for granted and question everything."[54]

The image Jaspers leaves us with, then, is not that of a man secure in the knowledge of Transcendence either in terms of a content which he can pass on or in the sense of a mystical oneness which is achieved apart from others. On the contrary, the image is that of men struggling, seeking along with others, always on the way. This is the struggle of thinking or philosophizing in which man knows himself to be related not to "the holy chain of 'witnesses to the Truth,' . . . nor to that of atheism . . . but rather . . . to the chain of private men who openly search in freedom."[55] This

52. *Wahrheit*, pp. 370 ff.; *Reason*, pp. 77 ff.
53. Fritz Kaufmann, "A Philosophy of Communication," *The Philosophy of Karl Jaspers*, p. 218, n. 25.
54. *Wisdom*, p. 26.
55. *Reason*, p. 141; see also Jaspers, *Reason and Anti-Reason in Our Time* (London: S.C.M. Press, 1952, and New Haven: Yale Univ. Press, 1952), p. 43.

struggle does not demand the abandonment of one's historicity and the fulfilment of one's life, but a struggle with the historically different in abandonment of all claims to exclusiveness. It is in this struggle that the limits to finite truth are realized and the openness to transcendent truth is made possible.[56]

In any literal sense then, Transcendence remains incommunicable. It is that which lies at the limits of our knowledge of the world and flashes out only momentarily in the moment of one's Existenz. Such an illumination is transitory and can never be drawn into the modes of thought without being lost. Yet man is not, according to Jaspers, resigned to silence, for it is the nature of communication to illuminate the realm of existence in such a way as to indicate its limits and open us up to Transcendence.[57] In this sense communication may be said to lie between Existenz and Transcendence as that which makes both a reality.

It follows that the task of philosophical faith in communication cannot be that of a direct transmission of truth. Its task is more of an enlightenment whose ultimate purpose is one of leading Existenz into an openness for Transcendence. Through clarifying the modes of the Encompassing, it illuminates the limits and consequently the possibilities of Existenz which can be fulfilled only in the individual moment in which man affirms himself in relation to the transcendent. It is true, of course, that men converse with each other in objective terms and that these terms cannot be identified with the truth of Transcendence without losing it. But it is possible, according to Jaspers, to speak in objective categories in such a way that we illuminate our failure to transmit the truth in which we participate. "I can only speak of that out of which I live and am, insofar as I miss saying it conceptually and therefore indirectly reveal it."[58]

In practice, then, the mode of communication is that of a joint inquiry in which the limits and incompleteness of truth in the

---

56. *Perennial Scope*, pp. 156 ff.; *Reason*, pp. 91–92.
57. *Reason*, pp. 105–106.   58. *Ibid.*, p. 122.

world are indicated. Every form of finite truth must be ship-wrecked in the world for "from the unfulfillment of every sense of truth and under the assumption that truth must be, thought touches upon Transcendence. . . . The unfulfillment of communi-cation and the difficulty of bearing its shipwreck become the revelation of a depth which nothing other than Transcendence can fill. . . . Before Transcendence . . . the unfulfillment of communi-cation disappears as the temporal appearance of truth."[59] It is this task which Jaspers undertakes in clarifying the modes of the En-compassing-that-we-are, pointing ultimately to that depth in man's potential Existenz which fails to find fulfilment in the finite and may open itself to Transcendence.[60]

The movement of thought in communication has the form of bartering (*Miteinanderaustauschen*). And in this sense the form of communication comes nearer to dialogue than pronouncement. Indeed, if it were possible for the meaning of philosophizing to be put into a particular artistic form, it would be that of the dialogue. The truth of philosophical faith is that which emerges or develops in exchanges between men, in their questioning and answering. For Jaspers this is not merely an intellectual venture; it involves the lives of the persons who may affirm themselves in relation to Transcendence. Thus the aim of bartering is always the tran-scendent truth toward which reason and Existenz move, and this truth appears only indirectly in the whole of discussion and argument.[61]

Although Jaspers doubts if Plato has grasped adequately the existential element of truth, there is no doubt that he has learned much from him. He acknowledges that Plato also recognized that truth arises only between persons and that it cannot directly enter speech. Like Plato, Jaspers proposes a use of language in com-munication which does not dictate or destroy but promotes a joint inquiry. For Jaspers the truth disclosed in this inquiry is one which

59. *Ibid.*, pp. 98, 104.   61. *Ibid.*, pp. 393 ff.
60. *Philosophie*, pp. 338 ff.

is grasped and authenticated only in the life of the individual. And in order that this may take place the partners in the inquiry must be open to communication with each other.

However, because communication itself does not control truth and because truth appears only in the moment of individual Existenz, there is no single literary or linguistic form which is adequate to the whole range of existential communication. Its only form is that the question of communicability as such remains conscious. Communication may take any form and yet must not lose itself in that form. Its task is that of recapturing all tendencies toward flatness in all forms of thought, illuminating the manifoldness of Existenz which is possessed in no formula. It approaches Existenz and Transcendence and yet does not permit either to come to rest in a stable form. "We can speak objectively— and we men can not speak otherwise—about the absolutely non-objective only in forms which cancel themselves out as objective."[62]

In practice, then, communication is present or *may* be present in Jaspers' illumination of the limits of truth in empirical existence, consciousness-as-such, and spirit, and in the affirmation of belief in Existenz and Transcendence. The cipher way of looking at the symbols of Transcendence and Existenz may ultimately lead us to truth. In this way the objective mode of communication loses its objectivity precisely in the encounter of its meaning in which I acknowledge that which by its nature remains incommunicable except indirectly.

It is this which leads Jaspers to reject the role of the pastor as that of translating the myths or symbols of faith into a supposedly non-mythological language. According to Jaspers, the pastor's task is one of giving meaning to myths which are cogent in our time. But he is able to do this only as one who authentically participates in the reality of the myths. His role is that of awakening man to a sense of his finiteness and thereby assisting him in

62. *Reason*, p. 117.

arriving at the "certainty" of faith. "He makes the mythical world his own, and gives it present meaning, not with the help of the theories of philosophers and theologians, but by the genuineness and the depth of his own experience of faith."[63] What is important in this activity is not the correctness of historical research but the spirit of faith. "The only essential thing is to speak in such a way that, with the help of a text, a present content of faith should be disclosed, and be shared in communication."[64]

The transcendent God for Bultmann, as for Jaspers, is known only in the moment of concrete existence. Thus God cannot be passed on from one person to another in dogmas or creeds. Bultmann also agrees with Jaspers that God does not come to men in an intuitive experience which bypasses the world. Nevertheless, the mode of communication through which man confronts God is other than that presented by Jaspers. According to Bultmann the communication of God occurs in the proclamation of the Christian Church.

The preaching of the Church corresponds to Jaspers' indirect communication in that its purpose is not one of passing on information but of bringing man into an existential relationship with the transcendent God. Bultmann even acknowledges that philosophical instruction may take on indirectly the character of preaching. That is, it can clarify the meaning of human existence and can lead the hearer to a mode of self-reflection in which he is faced with the question of his authentic existence.[65] However, in contrast to this indirect form of communication Bultmann understands genuine preaching as a summons or address. It is "a declaration which addresses the hearer immediately and challenges him to a definite act."[66]

To Jaspers any suggestion that God is communicated directly in the proclamation of the Church speaks of idolatry, the identifying of the transcendent with the human. Yet the basis of Bult-

63. *Myth*, p. 35.   65. *G.V.*, III, p. 122.
64. *Ibid.*, p. 103.   66. *Ibid.*

mann's claim that God unveils himself in the words of the preacher is the paradox, "the Word become flesh." The authority of the proclamation is not the preacher but the Word of God heard in the words that are spoken.

> Authentic Christian preaching is that which claims to be the call of God through the mouth of man and, as the authority demands faith. It is its particular paradox that in it God's will is encountered in human words. This paradox is most clearly expressed in the Gospel of John. Here in all clarity the offence is made distinct, in which Jesus, a man, claims, as Revealer, to speak the Word of God. The words which he speaks are God's words; he does not speak out of himself alone. The prologue of the Gospel expresses the paradox in the sentence, "The Word became flesh." But this paradox is also valid for the Church's preaching. . . . The preaching of the Church has its meaning as the Word of God, for the preacher does not present his own view, does not admonish and comfort on his own authority, but transmits the Word of God as the authoritative Word.[67]

Communication in this sense is not the handing on of information which is to be digested by an observer. It is the announcement of an event—the unveiling—of God. The preacher preaches not himself nor his own ideas but God's Word. It is from this Word that the proclamation has its authority. This is the reason for Bultmann's program of demythologizing, not in order to make the Bible more reasonable, but in order to let the Word to which the Bible witnesses be disclosed as an event.

For this same reason, preaching as a means of communication should not be confused with the giving of ethical or doctrinal instruction. While teaching may be included within preaching, it is justified only when it points up a question in this or that area of life and the answers given in light of the Word of God. Preaching

67. *Ibid.*, p. 124.

is not the teaching of general truths but the proclamation of the
Word of God, which is grasped only as an occurrence in the life
of one who hears in faith.

In speaking of this Word the preacher points to the event in
which God enters history. Authentic preaching, says Bultmann, is
that which preaches Jesus Christ as Lord. It is a historical event
(*geschichtliche Tatsache*), the communication of a historical occurrence which is more than an observed fact. The appearance of
Jesus which took place in history set an end to it, and the preaching of this event is properly grasped "only when it is understood
as the call to see in the appearance of Jesus the end of the world."[68]

Thus the content of the Word is not something separate from
the actualization of the Word as encounter but is united with it.
Insofar as preaching points to the event of Jesus, it is not a
historical report (*historische Mitteilung*) which tells of Jesus' life
and deeds. Rather, it proclaims Jesus as the end of the world when
it proclaims him as Lord, so that the paradox of Jesus within the
world putting an end to it rules over the life of the hearer who,
living within the world, withdraws from dependence upon it.
Where the Word truly resounds, the end of the world is a present
reality to the hearer in such a way that he is faced with the decision whether he will belong to the old or the new world, whether
he will remain the old man or become a new man.[69]

This means that the Word as heard in the words of the preacher
is an address, a personal Word which is known only in the concrete existence of the hearer. It is analogous to the word addressed
from one person to another, a word over which the hearer has no
control and which establishes a relationship between the two persons. God discloses Himself only in the person's being drawn into
relation with Him. Thus the speech which can communicate the
full and direct meaning of this action is analogical speech which
conceives God's action as an analogue to the actions occurring
between men.[70]

68. *Ibid.*, p. 127.   70. *Mythology*, p. 68.
69. *Ibid.*, pp. 128–129.

In that it is God's Word which is heard in the words of the preacher, it has its own authority which transcends the authority of the preacher and demands the response of faith. That is, in the moment when the sermon is heard as God's Word the maieutic relationship between men is transcended. The hearer no longer seeks to decipher the symbols in order to grasp the meaning beyond the words, but confronts the Word within the words and responds in faith.[71]

Bultmann does not interpret this to mean that faith is a *sacrificium intellectus*. The proclamation is not a communication of general truths; it is an address, really an event in which the hearer is placed in a situation which demands a decision. But the decision itself requires an understanding of the self and is not merely a blind act of will. Nevertheless, the spoken word cannot, according to Bultmann, be validated from beyond the address itself. When Jaspers asks for a legitimation of the words of the speaker, Bultmann replies that this is possible only in that the hearer finds himself under the address.[72] Bultmann is saying, in other words, that since proclamation communicates not general truths but an event, there is no means of validating it except in the moment of hearing itself.

Jaspers is able to agree in part with Bultmann at this point. Like Bultmann, Jaspers acknowledges the limits of the intellect; he understands philosophical faith to transcend these limits in its relation to God. He agrees that the awareness of Transcendence is in some sense self-authenticating insofar as it is beyond proof by means of empirical knowledge. Jaspers also agrees with Bultmann that God does not have to justify Himself before man. Yet a problem remains for him and for us. It may be that we cannot question God, but we must, it would seem, question the words in which it is claimed God speaks. "It is not God who has to justify himself, but Paul and all those who followed him down to Luther, and on to the present."[73]

---

71. *G.V.*, III, pp. 123–124.   72. *Ibid.*, p. 207; *Myth*, pp. 69–70.
73. *Myth*, p. 81. See also pp. 42, 68–70.

We would agree that there is a necessary distinction between the truth that we contemplate with our intellect and that which is also personal for us. Yet even this personal truth is addressed to us through general conceptions. Bultmann admits to this. "Even if we do not speak of God in general terms but rather of His action here and now on us, we must speak in terms of general conceptions, for all of our language employs conceptions. . . ."[74] But if God's personal address comes to me through general conceptions, it seems that my understanding of these general conceptions is related in some way to my personal understanding of God's address to me.

Bultmann understands authentic preaching as the Word of God addressing man personally through the medium of human words. In this is the paradox that the call of God comes through the mouth of man. But if this is true, the Christian faith must take this paradox seriously. It cannot with Jaspers find only words and experiences so that it finally transcends these words and experiences coming to God at some doubtful sphere at the borders of the finite world. But neither may it speak in such a way that the human aspect of this paradox is overcome by an overpowering Word of God. If we seek to maintain the paradox of the divine speaking in the human, the human must be as real as the divine. This paradox does not contradict what is human (language, thought, etc.) but only man's reliance upon the human in such a way that he finds fulfilment in himself.

Bultmann is certainly correct to emphasize that faith understands the words of preaching as the occasion in which God himself addresses man. While the words alone convey no more than human experiences, it is the belief of the Christian Church that God's Word is heard in these words. It would seem, however, that the words themselves have some real relation to the Word of God. One does not claim that God's Word is heard through nonsense syllables. Bultmann's own work indicates that he believes certain

74. *Mythology*, pp. 66–67.

forms of speech to be inadequate to the communication of God's Word. If this is so, it would seem that the words themselves play an important role in the communication of God's Word.

Unless the words which are said to be the vehicle of God's Word for me are open to reflection and unless this reflection is bound up in a positive way with their role as mediator, it would seem that I am left in a state of subjectivity in which God's Word can be distinguished from other words only on the basis of numinous feelings which are private to me. If we are in any situation able to say this is God's Word and this is not, we speak not simply out of inwardness but out of a decision which is not separated from reflection upon the various claims to truth. While Bultmann is helpful in pointing out that neutral observation does not acknowledge God's Word, he misleads us when he leaves the impression that this form of judgment is something entirely different from and unrelated to the decision of the self in the moment of revelation. On the contrary, we would maintain that every personal decision is made within the general considerations of the theoretical self.

Language and Meaning

Jaspers' reluctance to form any objective speech of God is dramatized in his repeated rejection of revelation, which, according to him, objectifies Transcendence and reduces it to the level of the immanent. Apparently he can only understand the Christian faith as a dogmatism which somehow identifies God with a stable object in the world. For him, the object has significance only as it is seen at the boundary of human existence where the object loses its objectivity and becomes transparent to Transcendence. Jaspers' philosophy is characterized by man's foundering at the limits of existence where Transcendence can be touched, although it remains unknown except to the immediacy of Existenz which finds here the givenness of its authentic self. Transcendence cannot be communicated in the language of the world but only indirectly in man's foundering in objectivity.

Here at the boundary, Transcendence momentarily flashes out and yet remains incommunicable, for when it is communicated it is drawn into the modes of the Encompassing where it is lacking. "Its experience is absolutely historical, in time out beyond time."[75] Jaspers attempts to escape both the objectification of Transcendence in *Offenbarungsglaube* and the flight from the world in asceticism. The language of the cipher is the means by which he seeks to do this. He wants to maintain a complete openness to truth, which has no bounds within the objective order and at the same time a finality to truth which can be realized in concrete Existenz. But this results in a communication of truth which is essentially negative and empty.

75. *Reason*, p. 106.

Jaspers' language of the myth understood as cipher invites comparison with Ludwig Wittgenstein's references to the mystical in the last few pages of *Tractatus Logico-Philosophicus*. For while in this volume Wittgenstein limits meaningful language to the propositions of natural science, he seems to be able to affirm the mystical. "There are, indeed, things that cannot be put into words. They *make themselves manifest*. They are what is mystical."[76] The mystical in this case is defined as "Feeling the world as a limited whole . . . ."[77] It cannot be said and hence cannot be thought. Yet it does seem to have reference to a real occurrence in the life of the individual.

> We feel that even when *all possible* scientific questions have been answered, the problems of life remain completely untouched. Of course there are then no questions left, and this itself is the answer.

> The solution of the problem of life is seen in the vanishing of the problem. (Is not this the reason why those who have found after a long period of doubt that the sense of life became clear to them have then been unable to say what constituted that sense?)[78]

According to the *Tractatus*, questions that can be asked and answered are questions concerning the *how* of the world, questions open to the language and thought of science. But the mystical is concerned *that* the world exists, and neither the questions nor the answers concerning the "that" can be put into words.[79] Thus, the questions and the answers remain without meaning, and "what we cannot speak about we must pass over in silence."[80] It would seem, then, that while Wittgenstein does not ignore the feeling of the mystical, he finds it meaningless within the limits of language as outlined in the *Tractatus* and thus invites us to pass over it in silence.

76. Ludwig Wittgenstein, *Tractatus Logico-Philosophicus* (London: Routledge and Kegan Paul, and New York: Humanities Press, 1963), 6.522. References here and elsewhere are to the propositions as numbered by Wittgenstein.
77. *Ibid.*, 6.45.   79. *Ibid.*, 6.44, 6.5.
78. *Ibid.*, 6.52, 6.521.   80. *Ibid.*, 7.

Jaspers also finds language unable to speak about what Wittgenstein calls the mystical. Transcendence is beyond all thought and speech. All conceptuality is shipwrecked at the end of philosophical reflection where man stands in silence before the face of Being.

It is silence in the face of being. Speech ceases in the presence of that which is lost to us when it becomes object.

This ultimate can be attained only in the transcending of all thought. . . . Here thought must dissolve into radiance. Where there is no further question, there is also no answer. In the philosophical transcending of question and answer we arrive at the limit, at the stillness of being.[81]

The apparent relation between the thought of Jaspers and Wittgenstein with regard to silence in the face of the mystical is disrupted, however, when Jaspers maintains that in spite of this, finite reality mediates a real relationship between Transcendence and Existenz. At this point Jaspers is pushing us toward a more definite affirmation of transcendent Being as opposed to a feeling of the mystical. All conceptual forms still remain in movement unable to speak about Transcendence. But if one cannot speak directly about Transcendence, one can, according to Jaspers, circumscribe it in the myths and symbols of history, appealing to the self, asking it to transcend the limits of the subject-object dichotomy and to awaken to that which is manifested within it.

Transcendence does not in this sense have the meaning that is defined in scientific language. But it does have a meaning in pointing to the questionableness of existence. Here at least it indicates that man is not master of himself, that he confronts limits whenever he attempts to grasp fully and order his existence, that his authentic selfhood cannot be created by him but only received from beyond that which is subject to the limits of the finite.

Jaspers thus moves beyond the early Wittgenstein's references to the mystical, exemplifying a structure of language that closely

81. *Wisdom*, p. 49.

parallels that of traditional negative theology. But it also suffers the same limitations of the *via negativa*. For while it speaks definitely of something that is more than a purely subjective or emotive experience, always referring the self beyond its own existence, it fails to characterize Transcendence in any significant sense. Transcendence remains little more than a question at the limits of existence, and the appropriate stance at times seems to be not decision but indecision.

Bultmann does not stand very far from Jaspers at this point. Father Malevez says that Bultmann's theology is "absolutely silent about the God whom it urges us to worship. . . . God illuminates our existence, but he himself remains veiled."[82] Indeed, as is illustrated in the following paragraph, Bultmann often speaks in a language that might well have come from the pen of Jaspers.

> This mysterious power—the power which limits man and is master of him even when he thinks he is his own master—is God, the controller of man's future. . . . The power which sets a terminus to knowing and doing is God. . . . *It is God who makes man finite*, who makes a comedy of man's care, who allows his longing to miscarry, who casts him into solitude, who sets a terminus to his knowing and doing, who calls him to duty, and who gives the guilty over to torment. And yet at the same time it is God who forces man into life and drives him into care. . . . God is the enigmatic power beyond time, yet master of the temporal; beyond being yet working in it. . . . His *transcendence* is that of someone always having power over the temporal and the eternal: it is the transcendence of the power which creates and sets limits to our life—not that of a substance or a void with which the soul unites and into which it is swallowed up as it soars above the world in devotion, abstraction and ecstasy.[83]

82. L. Malevez, *The Christian Message and Myth* (London: S.C.M. Press, 1958, and Westminster, Md.: Newman Press, 1960), p. 156.
83. *Essays*, pp. 3–9.

Bultmann repeatedly tells us that the revelation of God brings us no new knowledge about God which is not available to the non-believer, and the non-believer's knowledge of God is always said to be a negative knowledge of what God is not.[84] God must be a hidden and mysterious God. Otherwise our lives would become static and closed off to their full experience, and the approach of humility and reverence which is essential to faith would be destroyed. To attempt, as some do, to turn this negative knowledge into a positive knowledge of God is to sin.[85]

However, language about God in this sense has reference to a general knowledge or language about God and is to be contrasted with analogical language of God which speaks of what God does to me here and now.[86] God is not only hidden but also revealed. In the picture of the crucified Christ faith is said to have an embodiment of the hidden and revealed wisdom of God.

> Is it *only* the depths, *only* hiddenness and mystery that constitute his being? . . . No, riddle and mystery lose their meaning if they are not loved for the sake of what lies behind them, . . . if we are not brought to want a revelation and indeed to long for one with all our hearts . . . . God the mysterious and hidden must at the same time be the one who is revealed. Not, of course, in a revelation that one can know, that could be grasped in words and propositions, that would be limited to formula and book and to space and time; but rather in a revelation that continually opens up new heights and depths and thus leads through darkness from clarity to clarity. . . . And do we not have a picture that concretely embodies all this and places before our very eyes all that we have been struggling so hard to say? Do we not have a picture in which God's hidden and revealed wisdom is embodied—the wisdom that is able to bring all of the demonic powers of darkness into its plan of salvation; that is able to create a noble life out of the agony of

84. *Ibid.*, pp. 11–12, 302, 304; *Existence*, pp. 27–30.
85. *Essays*, pp. 114 ff.   86. *Mythology*, p. 66.

death and forsakenness; that swallows death up in victory and transforms a crown of thorns into the crown of a king? Indeed we do have such a picture of promise and redemption in the picture of the crucified Christ. And the picture of the crucified one as the embodiment of the hidden and revealed wisdom of God may help us also to understand the mysteries with which we are presently struggling.[87]

Bultmann consistently refuses to speak of God as He is in Himself, choosing to follow his teacher Wilhelm Hermann, who maintained that we can speak of God only as He is for us. To put it another way, he maintains that Christian faith is not in a general principle but in a definite Word proclaimed to the believer in the event of Jesus Christ. This belief does not teach man a new concept of God but gives him the right to believe in the One in whom he would fain believe. That is, man may be aware of God in the sense that he seeks the ground of his freedom and his detachment in the concrete situations of life. But he does not know God as something really standing over against him, apart from His revelation of Himself. He cannot address Him as "Thou" unless God becomes "his God" in the personal address of His Word, which promises him forgiveness and at the same time tells him that the acknowledgement of the transcendent is real when it is at once a confession of sin and a plea for mercy.[88]

Bultmann apparently recognizes the problem that is reflected in the negative speech of Transcendence and seeks to pass beyond it in pointing to the event in revelation in which the speaker takes part. Such speech in Bultmann's terms could never be objectifying in the sense of equating observed events with the action of God. Nor could such speech be merely emotive or non-cognitive. It would be analogical.

It is clear from this that Bultmann is dissatisfied with a wholly negative speech about God. But what he is proposing as a solution

---

87. *Existence*, pp. 30–33.   88. *Essays*, pp. 11–12.

to the problem is not clear. Because language of God, as he understands it, seems to have no real basis in the general dimension of human experience in the world, it sounds at times as if it is only speech of a direct and unmediated intuition. If Bultmann is dissatisfied with Jaspers' tendency to separate the world and God in language, then he must show more clearly what the relation between the world and God is and what the result is for the language of faith.

Bultmann goes a long way toward this in indicating faith to be dependent upon the event of Jesus as the Christ. Whatever his inadequacies at this point, he at least maintains that faith is bound up with this event in time. The Christian faith speaks of a historical occurrence (*historische Ereignis*) which is understood in faith as the eschatological occurrence. Thus, whenever faith speaks, it must speak in such a way that an event in time is grasped as the eschatological event while also indicating that the eschatological event is rooted in time. Otherwise, historical faith will be replaced by either an intuitive event or submission to empirical or dogmatic claims.

But, to the extent that Bultmann fails to make this paradox of the Christian faith clear, he fails to escape the negativism of Jaspers' language of Transcendence. A language of the Christian faith must express itself in such a way that the eschatological occurrence is understood as a real occurrence in the world. Unless the worldly event itself has some meaningful relation to the revelatory event, it is difficult to see how we escape presenting faith as an intuitive experience which is ultimately separated from the world. At the same time it must be acknowledged that the occurrence in the world can be understood as the eschatological occurrence only in faith's hearing the Word within it. Thus, the language of faith must also disclose the inseparability of God's action in the world and man's response to it in faith. In this sense language of faith is confessional in structure in that it is disclosing a view of an event which is a reality only in faith.

Properly understood, language of faith is neither a mystical or otherworldly language about God nor a positivistic language about the world. Rather, it is a disclosing of the world as world in such a way that man may hear the Word of God within it. Gerhard Ebeling means something like this, I believe, when he says: "faith is concerned with the world, with human nature; and what it says of God, of the Beyond and of eternal life has no other point at all than to bring man and the world to expression as what they truly are."[89]

If this direction is followed, language of faith can never be placed into a dimension apart from the criticism of other views of the world. On the contrary, faith must address itself to these other views of the world, calling them into question and disclosing its own view. Faith does not necessarily assume an exclusive or dogmatic role in this task. But it does speak with conviction out of its own confrontation with the world understood as God's creation. In this speaking, faith is both understanding and disclosing to others the truth through which it is determined. It cannot ignore the world's suggesting that God acts in some other dimension. But in speaking of the world it might bring it to expression as God's world.

89. Ebeling, *Word and Faith*, pp. 377–378.

IV Faith and Truth

Faith and Science

One of the contributions of philosophy and theology in this century has been the clarification of faith as a distinctive dimension of human experience. However, along with this contribution has come the tendency to separate faith from all forms of veridical judgment. To the extent that this is true the significance of faith is called into question. For if faith is beyond the scope of all validating inquiries, it is doubtful whether it has reference to anything that has a right to be spoken of as true or real. In what sense faith in either Jaspers' or Bultmann's sense has this tendency may be indicated by referring their views of faith to their views of other spheres of judgment, namely, to science, reason, and historical tradition.

According to Jaspers, the truth of philosophy and hence of philosophical faith is other than the truth of science. Science makes judgments on the basis of empirical evidence and requires no personal commitment in order that its knowledge be accepted as universally valid. Its discoveries are made on the basis of trial hypotheses which are confirmed or rejected through experience. But the truth of philosophy cannot stand alone on the basis of empirical evidence. It requires the commitment of the individual. That is, its truth is not demonstrable in the sense that truth is for science.

This does not mean, however, that a radical division exists between the knowledge of science and the knowledge of philosophy so that no positive relationship between them is possible. Rather, there are both positive and negative aspects to the relation between the knowledge of science and philosophy. Jaspers summarizes this relationship when he says that "philosophy cannot fully realize its possibilities except side by side with science, in distinction from science, and in aiming beyond science."[1]

First, then, philosophy may be said to stand side by side with science. That is, it never ignores the realities which are accessible to science and demands with it to know what is real. Such knowledge preserves the sanity of philosophical thought and makes it face the facts. "Unless an idea is submitted to the coldly dispassionate test of scientific inquiry, it is rapidly consumed in the fire of emotions and passions, or else it withers into a dry and narrow fanaticism."[2] Science is able to unmask illusions and break up false knowledge. It faces the half-truths that veil the realities from which man flees, and in breaking up premature and uncritical thinking, keeps man from falling into a deceptive complacency.

In this way science may be said to supply a method and attitude which is basic to philosophical inquiry. "Science springs from honesty and produces it."[3] It is honest in accepting the criticisms of its assertions and it compels one to examine one's insights. This is the honesty, according to Jaspers, which was essential to philosophers such as Sören Kierkegaard and Friedrich Nietzsche. It makes up that part of the scientific mode of thought which is "indispensable to the preservation of human dignity."[4] Second, philosophy recognizes that it is something distinct from science. In contrast to science's way of thinking, there is that type of thinking which "produces insights without universal validity and cogency, yet of fundamental importance to life itself."[5] Philosophical thinking penetrates through to the heart of reality that lies at the ground of all appearances. It is not concerned with something that is hitherto unknown, but is concerned to elucidate what one really wants, means, or believes. This truth does not stand alone on the basis of

1. Jaspers, *The Idea of the University* (Boston: Beacon Press, 1959), pp. 12–13.
2. *Wisdom*, p. 159.   4. *Ibid.*, p. 26.
3. *The Idea of the University*, p. 23.   5. *Ibid.*, p. 11.

rational judgment; it demands the commitment of the thinker. It is less than science in that it is not universally valid in the scientific sense; it is more than science in that it involves a creative way of thinking that actually transforms man.

Third, philosophy passes beyond science. Science does not produce knowledge of Being itself. It can give only knowledge of particular appearances or objects within the finite order. It cannot provide life with its meaning or goals, its values or directions. Rather, in the midst of scientific thinking we may become aware of its limits and consequently of that which has its source in something other than that available to scientific investigation. We may become aware of striving toward a unity of the particular data of science. No one piece of knowledge satisfies us, and we experience an "unqualified will to know," the questioning of reason which compels us to look toward the oneness of reality. Science in this sense is not understood as an end in itself but as a part of that striving toward the whole of truth.[6]

Philosophy may therefore be understood as inherent in the very act of scientific research; it is the inner meaning that guides the methodical work of science. And when a person becomes conscious of this movement of reason, he is at the stage of philosophizing. Apart from this guidance of reason, science becomes meaningless correctness and aimless busyness. Philosophy thus passes beyond the limits of science without rejecting its validity. Its truth is realized only in transcending the limits of scientific inquiry. This means that while philosophy does not reject science it does speak of a truth which has no universal validity, which requires the commitment of the individual, and in this sense is "absolute for him who conquers it in historical actuality . . . ."[7]

The relationship between scientific and philosophical truth is that of a circle. Philosophical faith affirms the truth of philosophy in transcending the limits imposed on man by the empirical world and thus criticizes science when it claims absolute knowledge based on

6. *Ibid.*, pp. 14 ff.   7. *Wisdom*, p. 162.

the empirical world. At the same time, faith stands open to the findings of science if it wants to be other than uncritical fanaticism. Science criticizes the tendency in faith toward uncritical conclusions. Yet it acknowledges the limits that it faces in its own sphere and leaves the way open to philosophical faith.

The distinction between the knowledge of science and the knowledge of faith which is observed by Jaspers is also observed by Bultmann. According to Bultmann scientific knowledge arises out of the methodical investigation of phenomena which encounter man in the world. The object is understood as it is in itself, and a commitment of the investigator is not essential to knowledge of it. Faith's knowledge in contrast requires the commitment of the knower. It is that which is grasped by man in the reality of the moment. Faith's knowledge is that of the will and the responsiveness in the moment. It involves a decision which cannot be replaced by scientific investigation.[8]

This does not mean, however, that faith denies the validity of scientific investigation. On the contrary, faith is said to free man for this activity. The Christian faith in fact demands this form of knowledge. Christian existence is eschatological. Man is not bound by the world and yet he lives in it. And so long as man makes his life in the world of concrete and practical concerns, he requires the scientific knowledge which is vital to life in this world.[9]

In this regard faith does not contradict the scientific view of the world but accepts it as essential to life. It is on this basis that the mythological view of the world may be said to be obsolete. The believer does not have the freedom to invent his own world view. This is a part of his inherited situation in history, and if he wishes to debate the established world view, it must be from within the realm informed by science. In other words, faith does not suggest a competing view of the world but only maintains that science does not comprehend the whole of reality.[10]

8. *G.V.*, III, pp. 107 ff.   9. *Essays*, pp. 87 ff.
10. *Mythology*, p. 61; *Essays*, pp. 88–89.

Bultmann's understanding of the Christian faith is therefore not one which brings faith into conflict with the discoveries of natural science. As a theologian he is only concerned that science recognize its limits, that it remain secular and not attempt to suggest the meaning and purpose of being. The conflict between faith and science arises only when the latter claims on the basis of the "knowable" to possess the meaning of human existence. Under these conditions science is replaced by "scientism" and holds out to man a mistaken sense of security which has its basis in man's thinking himself master of the world.

The Christian faith, then, does not reject scientific explanation. Its paradox lies not in a view of the world that conflicts with empirical investigation but in the fact that it "understands as God's action here and now an event which is completely intelligible in the natural or historical connection of events."[11] God's action in the world is hidden except to the eye of faith and is not subject to the control of empirical investigation. The believer may speak of an act of God only in relation to his existence and never in such a way as to identify observed events with the divine.

In this manner Bultmann makes the distinction between science and faith which permits each to recognize that it has its own dimension of concern. He does not seem, however, to have done much more than this. Bultmann contributes to what John Habgood has called "the uneasy truce between science and theology," but he makes no serious effort to suggest how science and faith might also be related.[12] The risks connected with the failure to indicate a positive relation between them are many, and it is beyond the scope of this study to investigate them in any detail. Still, it is clear that concentration on the differences between science and faith to the neglect of their relationships will result in an attitude in which God's action is understood to have no reality in the

11. *Mythology*, p. 65.
12. John Habgood, "The Uneasy Truce between Science and Theology," *Soundings: Essays Concerning Christian Understanding*, ed. A. R. Vidler (Cambridge: Cambridge Univ. Press, 1962), pp. 21 ff.

world. There will be a tendency for the secular to be reduced to ideologies of one sort or another and for faith to be placed into an irrelevant sphere, to be treated as the product of one's private needs and emotions.

Occasionally Bultmann does hint that there is a more positive side to the relation between science and faith. In practice he shows that faith can be open to science's criticism of its mythology, and he does say in at least one place that science leads faith to reflect on its true nature.[13] He also points to something like Jaspers' suggestion that science and faith have a common ground in the total search of reason when he comments regarding the forms of human community:

> In all of this, of course, the possibility of true community is always there—in the sphere of engineering as the possibility of comradeship; and in the sphere of science it will be to a great extent realized the more the research worker as a man has a part *existentiell-ly* in the subject which gives his work its validity; that is, the more he is aware of the fact that all scientific work is ultimately not intended to bring to light partial truths, but that it takes place in the service of the search for the truth about man's existence—in the service of a true understanding of the self. I need only call in mind names like Planck and von Weizsäcker.[14]

Nevertheless, Bultmann is usually silent on the subject of a positive relation between faith and science. In itself this silence might not be taken as such a problem. But when it is coupled with the fact that he tends to separate faith from rational criticism (as is indicated in the next section), it is symptomatic of a serious problem, since he is wanting to address contemporary man whose honest secularity does not permit him to treat faith as anything real if it has no connection with the rest of his life.

13. *Kerygma and Myth* (London, 1957), p. 4; *Essays*, p. 19.
14. *Essays*, p. 299.

Faith and Reason

The role of reason in its attempt to understand the self and its relation to reality has come to play an increasingly significant part in the development of Jaspers' philosophy. He now prefers to speak of his philosophy in terms of reason rather than in terms of existence.[15] Yet reason as he understands it is not a polar opposite to philosophical faith. It seems in fact that there has been a parallel development of reason and faith in his thought.

Reason (*Vernunft*) refers to that movement in human existence which "takes in" all various meanings of truth. It is bound up with existence and develops in relation to it. Reason seeks all possibilities open to existence with the aim of embracing the whole of truth. In this process no one truth is complete in itself and no one truth can claim final authority. Reason asserts each truth but follows at the same time an underlying and inextinguishable urge toward the One where all belongs to all.

Reason then exemplifies a "will to unity" or a "will to the One." Yet it refuses to settle upon any single unity in such a way as to produce a completed system of truth. It always refuses final harmonization and strives to effect a breakthrough in every totality. It is open to the infinity of meaningful content and breaks through every fixation of truth in order to stand open to that which is more than any particular truth.[16]

Reason which stands open to the infinity of meaningful content is not a natural endowment which acts without choice in our being. It is based upon a decision. By a free act man takes up the life of

---

15. "Reply to My Critics," p. 838.
16. *Offenbarung*, pp. 126 ff.; *Wahrheit*, p. 120; *Perennial Scope*, pp. 45 ff.

reason. That he can do this is a mystery to him, for according to Jaspers, he is aware that he cannot create this freedom; it must be a gift to him. Thus the decision for reason is simultaneously a decision for truth, freedom, and the unconditionality of the decision. It stands over against the limits of natural necessity.[17]

Reason, understood in this sense, is not an enemy of the philosophical faith but an indispensable element in it. Reasoning man lives out of the roots of his particular history while relating to every particular mode of historicity that he encounters.[18] He breaks through the limits of all particular histories in recognizing an all-encompassing unity beyond them. Here, the possibility of a consciousness of that which transcends all particulars is disclosed. Philosophical faith affirms the way of reason and acts within it in such a way that man overcomes his empirical isolation and acknowledges that the source of his being comes from beyond himself. This is an act which must be continually undertaken in man's coming to his authentic self in the moment.[19]

This does not mean, however, that reason and philosophical faith are free from the challenge of the understanding (*Verstand*), the "intellectual" or objective understanding that takes place in the isolating of ideas. On the contrary, reason and understanding are rooted in the same being and as such are in continuous dialogue. Reason can make no move without the critique of the understanding; it must undergo at every turn man's attempt at definiteness and clarity. The understanding challenges reason by fixing limits and striving for clarity and certainty. And in turn reason challenges the understanding, allowing it to come to rest in no certain knowledge, breaking through its conclusions in recognition of their limits.[20]

Jaspers does not make the error associated with the Enlightenment. He is aware of the misuse of the understanding which bases

17. Jaspers, *Reason and Anti-Reason in Our Time*, pp. 50 ff.
18. *Perennial Scope*, pp. 42–46.
19. *Reason*, pp. 141 ff.
20. *Wahrheit*, p. 120; *Offenbarung*, p. 128.

all knowledge, will, and action upon it alone. This is the false use of the understanding which destroys the tradition upon which all life exists. It destroys faith and results in nihilism. When misunderstood in this sense, the understanding seeks to absolutize its insights, which in fact can never be more than particular and hence less than absolute.[21]

Misconceived, the understanding is an enemy of faith. But when its limits are recognized, it becomes an essential factor in the comprehension and elucidation of philosophical faith. The challenge of the understanding is directed against all forms of blindness which accept ideas without questioning them. It stands over against all restrictions to inquiry and all traditional prejudices. It demands an unlimited critical awareness of the quality and limit of every insight. With this faculty man strives to understand what he believes; he wants to base his knowledge on experience fundamentally accessible to all. He wants to know the degree to which proof is valid and the limits where the intellect is frustrated. "And he would like also to have a reasoned basis for the indemonstrable premise, which he must ultimately take as the foundation of his life . . . ."[22]

Philosophical faith stands in the midst of the dialogue between reason and understanding. Reason seeks the limits of knowledge and opens the way for faith to transcend the empirical isolation of man. But this faith must always be subjected to the critical questioning of the intellect. It is in this dialogue between reason and understanding that faith is possible, and it is here that philosophical faith is indicated to be something other than a subjective creation of man.

Bultmann has been more ambiguous than Jaspers in indicating the relation between reason and faith. He does distinguish his attitude toward reason and faith from one that would demand the sacrifice of our life on the intellectual plane. And in keeping with his interpretation of Paul he makes a place for reason as inquiry

21. *Wisdom*, pp. 89 ff.   22. *Ibid.*, p. 88.

into the meaningful structures of reality, distinguishing between the inquiry itself and evil will which struggles for dominance of reason. But Bultmann also speaks at times in a manner which suggests that reason and faith operate on two different levels having little or no essential relation to each other.[23]

Reason, understood as the source of meaning in human existence, can be observed in Bultmann's discussion of the inquiry of existence. According to Bultmann, "Every human being knows or can know about its finiteness . . . ."[24] Human existence is moved by its "care" for the morrow and yet knows that it cannot make life secure within its limited means. Life is driven this way and that way, longing for the true and the beautiful, the meaning of life. It is motivated by the desire for love or the thirst for knowledge in which one admits that one can know nothing. Life is driven by the idea of deity and hears the summons of the ought. There is a kind of knowledge we confront in this experience, although it is "not theoretical knowledge but is the knowledge which breaks in on us in critical moments of our being itself."[25]

Reason understood in this sense gives rise to the intellectual pursuits of the human mind; thus intellectual investigations are not to be avoided. Bultmann has himself contributed to the realm of the intellect in his work as a historical critic, and he explicitly acknowledges the importance of scientific knowledge in the interpretation of the Bible and in the clarification of faith. Intellectual pursuits are necessary insofar as man must preserve his faith in the active life of the world in which he is to be master in God's service.[26]

However, according to Bultmann, intellectual pursuits, which are associated with humanism, result in the attempt to *"make the world man's home."*[27] Science, law, and art lead man to look on himself as a member of the cosmos, which he perceives as an

---

23. *Essays*, p. 51; Bultmann, *This World and the Beyond* (London: Lutterworth Press, 1960, and New York: Scribner's, 1960), pp. 157 ff.

24. *Essays*, p. 2.   26. *Ibid.*, pp. 19, 161 ff.

25. *Ibid.*, p. 7.   27. *Ibid.*, p. 152.

entity pervaded by his mind. And to the extent that man becomes content with this world and his place in it faith contradicts it. "In the eyes of the Christian faith the world is the extraneous element, which even the dominion of the mind cannot turn into a home."[28] The world is not man's home and cannot be turned into such on the basis of a civilization set up in the service of the true, the good, and the beautiful. Faith speaks of a God who is not known in man's striving for the true, the good, and the beautiful but only in man's being freed from the limits of this striving.

Bultmann then does not simply reject either the inquiry of reason or the investigations of the understanding. Yet he does very little to clarify the positive contribution of the understanding in relation to faith except to say that it is necessary to the life of the believer who must live in the world. On the contrary, he assumes that man does not in fact remain in open inquiry about God, that he twists a negative knowledge of God into a positive knowledge and thus secures himself in the world in which he lives. He makes the world his home.[29]

It is this which makes his reader suspicious of his attempt to suggest that faith is not a *sacrificium intellectus*.[30] Bultmann really seems to suggest that the understanding works on a different level from faith and has very little to do with it. Thus, the Word of God is said to be addressed to the self as a hearer but not to the theoretical reason.[31] Faith requires the understanding in living in the world, but the understanding apparently has no capacity for challenging faith, which is in a different dimension. And even if we claim that Bultmann implicitly at times accepts the challenge of the understanding to faith, he does not develop it explicitly and on some occasions seems openly to reject its criticism. This has led persons such as H. P. Owen and Ronald Hepburn to say that Bultmann makes a deficient assessment of human reason.[32] Owen and

28. *Ibid.*, p. 153.   29. *Ibid.*, pp. 114–115.
30. *This World and the Beyond*, pp. 157–158; *Mythology*, p. 36.
31. *Mythology*, p. 36.
32. Owen, *Revelation and Existence*, pp. 147 ff.; Hepburn, "Demythologizing and the Problem of Validity," pp. 230 ff.

Hepburn cite similar passages in support of their criticism, two of which are given below:

> The man who wishes to believe in God as his God must realize that he has nothing in his hand on which to base his faith. He is suspended in mid-air, and cannot demand a proof of the Word which addresses him. For the ground and object of faith are identical. Security can be found only by abandoning all security, by being ready, as Luther put it, to plunge into the inner darkness.[33]
>
> It would be wrong at this point to raise again the problem of how this preaching arose historically, as though that could vindicate its truth. That would be to tie our faith in the word of God to the results of historical research. The word of preaching confronts us as the word of God. It is not for us to question its credentials. It is we who are questioned, we who are asked whether we will believe the word or reject it.[34]

The basis for Owen's and Hepburn's criticism that Bultmann makes an insufficient assessment of reason is brought into even clearer focus in Bultmann's essay, "How Does God Speak to Us through the Bible." The following paragraphs are taken from it:

> For what God says to us through the Bible is in the form of *address*. It can only be listened to, not examined. The man to whom God really speaks through the Bible hears what God says to him and acts accordingly, and he has just as little time and reason to ponder over the *how*, as has a son to submit the style of his father's words to theoretical examinations. In doing so, he would forget to hear rightly . . . .
>
> How then should we hear? Which is the right way to prepare? The first condition for readiness is this: we must silence all other voices; everything we say to ourselves, everything other people say to us. For we want to hear what *God* says to

33. *Kerygma and Myth* (London, 1957), p. 211.
34. *Ibid.*, p. 41.

us. And if we take this seriously, there is room for but one voice. . . .

Is that possible? Is the promise of the Scriptures that God has forgiven us and received us in his mercy through Jesus Christ a word that we can believe as God's word?

If we still ask these questions, we are obviously not yet rightly prepared. For they indicate that we still consider the Bible as an ordinary book which we may study like other books in order to profit by it. If we ask for plain convincing reasons why God speaks actually here, in the Bible, then we have not yet understood what God's sovereignty means.[35]

The problem suggested by Owen and Hepburn and by the passages cited here is an important one which has already arisen in several contexts in this study. When Bultmann refers to natural revelation, to the translation of mythology into existential concepts, and to scientific investigations, he appears to be indicating a positive relation between faith and the rational activities of man. But when he then refuses to discuss a criterion of revelation with Jaspers, and when he suggests that we must silence all other voices in hearing the Word of God, he seems to be demanding that we place faith and man's rational inquiry into two unrelated dimensions of experience.

What then is the source of this problem? It lies first of all in Bultmann's failure to develop clearly the relationship between reason and understanding. While he indicates a definite awareness of both the receptive and the critical functions of man's rational being, he does not seem to have a clear idea of the critical functioning of the understanding in reason's inquiry about God. He concentrates on that aspect of the inquiry which passes beyond the limits of finiteness and objectivity and opens itself up to the revelation of God. However, a complete analysis of the movement of reason demands an awareness of the critical function of reason in

35. *Existence*, pp. 166–168.

every act. In other words, reason and understanding are not in the last analysis two unrelated dimensions of human experience. Man does not come to the Bible in such a way that he sets aside his critical reflection. On the contrary, it is only in the midst of his criticism of the objective structures before him and in reason's seeking to transcend the limits indicated by the understanding that God's Word has any meaning. Just because God's Word encounters man from within some objective form, faith can never bypass reflection on that form.

Second, there is the tendency in Bultmann's thought for the understanding and the decision of faith to be treated as if they were really unrelated. Thus he writes:

> Christian preaching, in so far as it is preaching of the Word of God by God's command and in His name, does not offer a doctrine which can be accepted either by reason or by a *sacrificium intellectus*. Christian preaching is kerygma, that is, a proclamation addressed not to the theoretical reason, but to the hearer as a self.[36]

According to Bultmann, human life is lived through decisions, and this means in contrast to the thought of Croce that man is essentially will, although Bultmann admits that will is in general not without reason.[37] In practice this definition of man leads Bultmann to speak of decision as if it were divorced from the theoretical reason. However, a more realistic appraisal of man's condition would seem to suggest that in every decision which is other than blind impulse (which after all is no decision) there is an element of withdrawal, a questioning which, if it can never prove the validity of faith's decision, does challenge the tendency of faith to find its security in the world or in human subjectivity. This does not mean that reasoning results in a form of abstract disinterested objectivity but that reasoning is vitally bound up with one's commitment.

This is not to suggest that Bultmann errs in emphasizing the fact

36. *Mythology*, p. 36.
37. *History and Eschatology*, p. 142.

that one cannot legitimate the Word of God by applying one's understanding to the Bible, the sermon, and so on. Such an assertion would require that one submit to the authority of the understanding and remain blind to its limits. Nevertheless, because the understanding is a part of the self addressed by the Word of God, one cannot speak as if to set aside the questioning of the understanding. Rather, it is in the struggle of the understanding that human limits are revealed and God is indicated to be possible as something other than an object in the world. It is this struggle, so to speak, which prepares the way for faith, or better, in the struggle of reason and understanding faith comes to itself before the address of God. And since faith is new in every situation, human existence must be understood in a dialectic of questioning and faith in every moment.

Faith and Tradition

Philosophical faith is realized in the life of the exception, that is, in the life of one who struggles against all forms of objective authority. Yet it is only in relation to the perceptible authority of the world, the tradition, that faith has its birth. Thus, philosophical faith exists amid the polarity of authority and the exception. The authority of tradition represents the becoming immanent of Transcendence, and the life of the exception represents the refusal to permit Transcendence to be lost in the immanent world. In this relation to tradition as we seek its source and find our own source we become our authentic selves.[38]

Philosophical faith, then, is dialectically related to historical tradition. Tradition provides no authority or security to faith; it is not an objective truth to be substituted for direct relationship with Transcendence. All traditions are bound to time and give us neither fellowship nor a guarantee. No tradition contains a universally valid truth which is acceptable to philosophical faith. "Nowhere is the truth ready made; it is an inexhaustible stream that flows from the history of philosophy as a whole from China to the West, yet flows only when the primal source is captured for new realizations in the present."[39] The truth of faith is in the final analysis dependent upon the selfhood of the believer who confronts this truth in the seeking of the transcendent source of tradition without succumbing to its objective manifestations in obedience and service.

Philosophical faith is free from tradition in the sense that tradition is not an authority for it. Nevertheless, faith is not constructed

38. *Wahrheit*, pp. 766 ff.   39. *Perennial Scope*, pp. 21–22.

by the believer out of his own subjectivity but grows out of his relation to his whole tradition extending from the last millenium B.C. to the present day. "Beginning with his own proximate tradition in family, home country, people, rooted in his own past, the philosopher broadens and deepens it, extending his scope to the vast worlds of the West and thence to all mankind, until finally he consciously finds the pivot of the whole in the epoch between 800 and 200 B.C."[40] The historical tradition is therefore not important to faith as its guarantee but as the language in relation to which faith comes to itself. The individual studies the historical tradition and gains an intelligent mastery of the facts. But objective historical knowledge itself is not adequate to faith. Such knowledge must be transcended until the investigator personally experiences the source of his own being. The historical tradition thus becomes the mirror of what is his own, and he comes to himself in his present experience. Philosophy has only one reality, says Jaspers, and that is here and now. It is only through this present reality that we gain access to the timeless.[41]

Thus, while Jaspers finds some analogy between the authority of tradition for philosophical faith and the authority of tradition for religious faith, he is careful to emphasize that in philosophy tradition does not demand obedience. Authority can be a source of truth only when it has its source in the Encompassing, that is, in all modes of the Encompassing. But the unity of all modes of the Encompassing is something never fulfilled in time. The historical tradition is looked upon as the deposit of inexhaustible truth, which is a source by which we come to the truth in our experience, but it can never claim to be a definitive truth that requires our obedience.[42]

Tradition is that in relation to which we may awaken to truth as we break through its objectifications and approach its ultimate source, which is also the source of our being. Thus there is no one

---

40. *Ibid.*, pp. 115–117.   41. *Wisdom*, pp. 142–144.
42. *Wahrheit*, pp. 769 ff.; *Wisdom*, pp. 142–143.

historical tradition which demands obedience. Philosophical faith is able to look upon the many authorities or traditions as appearances of the one transcendent authority which is never fulfilled in a timely reality. "Every tradition is valid as a possible language, and becomes a true language . . . in given historical situations for Existenz, which discovers itself in them."[43] When the authority shipwrecks in its historical forms, the truth which is its source may be disclosed.

In this capacity of "awakener" Jaspers accepts the Bible as an important source for Westerners. Although the Bible is not a source for universally valid ideas, it is a historical source before which the illumination of the self can take place. The Bible is a depository of human experiences of Transcendence. It includes the religious, mythical, historical, and existential experiences of men over a thousand years. What is spoken of as revelation is therein already interpretation in human speech and thought.[44]

The results of biblical study then include not only historical (*historisch*) knowledge, but also the assimilation of the reality which lies at its source and can become known in man's personal relation to it. In reflection man grasps the existential meaning of the Bible, winning what is "non-historical" in the historical facts. In this reflection he may become open to that which lies at the source of the biblical record but cannot be contained in finite categories.[45]

However, while Jaspers emphasizes the importance of the biblical tradition and what he understands to be the biblical religion, he also contends that philosophy goes beyond it in a boundless communication which sets all traditions in relation to each other. Philosophical faith binds itself to no one tradition; it extends itself without limit, opening itself up to the truth of all traditions. Because of this no one tradition and no combination of them have real authority for it. True authority remains unfixed, always subject

43. *Myth*, p. 47; see also *Wahrheit*, pp. 783 ff.
44. *Offenbarung*, pp. 490 ff.   45. *Ibid.*, pp. 492–493.

to change by a more thorough understanding of itself in communication with other authorities.[46] Traditions are important insofar as one awakens to one's source of being in dialogue with them. But there is no equivalent in philosophical faith to the authority of tradition found in religious faith. The historical tradition does not guarantee the truth of faith but is a cipher by which one awakens to Transcendence in the moment.[47]

When Jaspers asks the question, "Where does God speak to us?" he answers that God speaks "directly to individuals in the truth which tradition can only awaken and prepare us to hear. It speaks in the freedom of self-existence as the medium in which man . . . must be God-given to himself, to be really human." And he contrasts this answer with that given by religion in which God speaks "only through the medium of revelation (a past occurrence transmitted to us by such human institutions as the Church, in cults and sacraments and phrases of human languages, i.e., always by worldly realities), through authority and obedience."[48] Thus, while philosophical faith speaks without claim to authority, depending on persuasion, religious faith, according to him, conveys an assurance of faith backed up by an objective guarantee.

Bultmann finds neither of these options acceptable to Christian faith. To treat the historical tradition simply as an awakener to truth in such a way that the tradition itself is transcended is to ignore the historicity of man and faith as defined by Bultmann and ultimately to find the coincidence of subject and object outside history. In contrast, Christian faith is said to have an indissoluble relation with the historical tradition of the Christian Church. Yet the historical tradition itself is not understood as a guarantee for faith.

Bultmann makes this obvious in his discussion of faith and historical (*historisch*) investigation. Faith is the response to the

46. Jaspers, *Philosophy and the World* (Chicago: Regnery, 1963), pp. 48 ff.

47. *Perennial Scope*, pp. 114 ff.

48. Jaspers, *Existentialism and Humanism* (New York: R. F. Moore, 1952), pp. 93–94.

Word of God as made manifest in the proclamation of the Church. However, this does not mean that the Word of God is open to historical verification. While faith is in some way bound to the historical tradition, it is not bound in such a way that historical factuality verifies it. Manfred Hoffman echoes Bultmann's sentiments when he says that faith verified by historical factuality would be "the product of *homo faber* rather than the *creatio ex nihilo* of God (*sola fide*)."[49]

It is for this reason that Bultmann is skeptical of the so-called new quest for the historical Jesus. According to Bultmann it is not the historical Jesus but the Christ of the kerygma who is the object of faith, and man who is addressed by the kerygma may not go behind it seeking to verify it by historical investigation. The proclamation that God has acted in Jesus as the Christ can neither be affirmed nor denied by historical investigation because it is beyond the sphere of historical investigation to say that God has acted here. Ultimately this proclamation is authenticated only in the moment of revelation itself in which the believer becomes a new creature in Christ.[50]

This does not mean, however, that the historical tradition of the Christian faith is something that one may take or leave at will. To remove faith from the event of Jesus would, according to Bultmann, make faith into a system of general truths and hence destroy its historicity. In other words, faith has its being in history and not in some otherworldly sphere of eternal truths. In this context Bultmann speaks of the *Dass* of Jesus as "evidence" for the kerygma. *That* Jesus was is the necessary presupposition to the kerygma which proclaims that in Jesus God acts. Thus, the proclamation of the Christian Church is contingent upon the historical Jesus at least to the point of requiring his *Dass*. Without this *Dass* Christian faith would have no rootage in time, and faith would at the very least be radically altered.[51]

49. Manfred Hoffmann, "Kerygma and History," *Journal of Bible and Religion*, XXXIII, No. 1 (January, 1965), 27.
50. *Heidelberg Lecture*, pp. 12 ff.; *Essays*, p. 18; *History*, p. 151.
51. *Heidelberg Lecture*, pp. 7 ff.; *Kerygma and Myth* (London, 1957), pp. 115 ff.

In this manner, then, faith in the Word of God as confronted in the proclamation of the Church is bound to the coming of Jesus as the presupposition of the kerygma. For this reason, Bultmann could never say, as does Jaspers, that the preacher should learn what he can from the tradition and then set it aside in his practical relationships in the community.[52] Faith has its birth in the kerygma and consequently is bound up with the historical tradition of the Christian Church. But the only thing that historical research may verify in this connection is that Jesus of Nazareth is the presupposition of the Church's proclamation. It is the proclamation itself which proclaims the coming of Jesus as the Christ and presents this event as a concrete Word which puts my life in question and demands my response. In this way the past may become a present reality for me.[53]

Faith then has its birth in relation to the kerygma which proclaims God's act in Christ as an act for me. The real authority of faith is the Word of God as proclaimed in the kerygma. Yet unless the kerygma is to be treated as a cipher, we cannot ignore the fact that the kerygma makes use of words which in affirming one thing deny another. Consequently we cannot avoid asking whether these words have any reality in history or whether they are not purely arbitrary constructions. That is, if the kerygma proclaims an event in history, may we not expect, even demand, that there be continuity between the event and the words proclaiming the event? Otherwise, does not the kerygma become understood as a law which in some way defines and guarantees faith?

Bultmann is of little help at this point. We find him saying that the "reliability of the kerygmatic tradition must not be questioned" or that "the word of preaching confronts us as the word of God. It is not for us to question its credentials."[54] On another occasion Bultmann maintains that man is told in the Christian message that "in what happened then, whatever the circumstances, God has acted, and that through this action of his the Word of divine

---

52. *Myth*, p. 103.
53. *Kerygma and Myth* (London, 1957), p. 115.
54. *Ibid.*, pp. 116, 41.

judgement and of forgiveness which now confronts him is authenticated. . . ."[55] Or again, "The church's preaching, founded on
the Scriptures, passes on the word of the Scriptures. It says: God
speaks to you *here*! . . . We cannot question whether this place is
the right one; we must listen to the call that summons us."[56]

There is no doubt that the motivation for such statements is the
refusal to make the Word of God identical with rational knowledge.
Bultmann wants to say nothing that would make this Word something over which we have control. Further, he does not intend to
say that the kerygma is a law or dogma which demands our assent
in spite of ourselves. He quotes with approval Vahanian's suggestion that religious authority does not replace personal autonomy
with assent to a system of beliefs, that "religious authority . . .
symbolizes a synthesis of subjective truth and objective reality
. . . ."[57] The tradition in Bultmann's point of view is kerygmatic,
not legal or doctrinal. The Church as the bearer of the kerygma
proclaims an event of faith and demands submission to the event
of God's Word, not to doctrinal formulas. "The 'demythologized'
sense of the Christian doctrine of incarnation, of the word that 'was
made flesh' is precisely this, that God manifests himself not merely
as the idea of God—however true this idea may be—but as 'my'
God, who speaks to me here and now, through a human mouth."[58]

Nevertheless, the question remains, whether in fact Bultmann
has been able to escape the tendency to make the kerygma and
hence the tradition into a law or dogma. Certainly this is not his
intention. He himself warns us that apart from the concrete situation of the life of the speaker the teachings of Jesus would be no
more than general truths. And yet he consistently refuses to say
any more historically about the kerygma than that it presupposes
the person of Jesus. Bultmann does say in his Heidelberg lecture
that Jesus is really present in the kerygma. But Bornkamm points

55. *Essays*, p. 18.   56. *Existence*, p. 168.
57. Bultmann, "Der Gottesgedanke und der moderne Mensch," *Zeitschrift
für Theologie und Kirche*, 60 (December, 1963), p. 343; Gabriel Vahanian,
The Dealth of God: The Culture of Our Post-Christian Era (New York:
George Braziller, 1961), p. 164.
58. *Myth*, p. 70.

up the problem in this when he says that if we ignore the what and how of Jesus' life, he is present only as a mere fact of salvation and not as a person.[59] In other words, if we eliminate or show inadequately the continuity between the person of Jesus and the proclamation about him, we lose the concreteness of God's act and substitute for it a dogma with no apparent basis in reality.

Bultmann is faced with an important decision at this point if he wants to avoid making the kerygma into a dogma announced by the tradition and requiring obedience. Either he must treat the kerygmatic tradition as one cipher among others whose content is not in the final analysis important to faith, or he must develop more adequately the sense in which the kerygma is concretized in the persons of Jesus. Paul Althaus is suggesting this when he says: "The *kerygma* is a statement, a dogma, if we do not see it filled out by the living picture of Jesus as the gospels portray Him."[60] The kerygma properly understood directs me to a concrete event in time in which God's Word is addressed to me, not to a set of assertions which seem on occasion to be separated from the event.

Bultmann has made it clear that he does not wish to follow in the direction indicated by Jaspers. Yet his development in the other direction is inadequate. The primary reason for his resistance to the development of his thought in the direction suggested by Bornkamm, Althaus, Ebeling, and others seems to be that he does not want to falsify the claim that the kerygma is not subject to verification by way of historical research. Yet these theologians have repeatedly emphasized their agreement at this point.[61] They do not claim that we need to prove the kerygma or that such is even possi-

---

59. Gunter Bornkamm, "Mythos und Evangelium," *Theologische Existenz Heute*, XXVI (1951), 18. Cited in Paul Althaus, *Fact and Faith in the Kerygma of Today*, trans. David Cairns (London: Oliver and Boyd, and Philadelphia: Muhlenberg, 1959), p. 45.

60. Althaus, *Fact and Faith*, pp. 45–46; see also Gerhard Ebeling, *Theologie und Verkündigung, Ein Gesprach mit Rudolf Bultmann* (Tübingen: J.C.B. Mohr [Paul Siebeck], 1962), pp. 68 ff.

61. Althaus, *Fact and Faith*, pp. 60 ff.; Gunther Bornkamm, *Jesus of Nazareth*, trans. Irene and Fraser McLoskey with James Robinson (New York: Harper and Row, and London: Hodder and Stroughton, 1960), p. 9; James Robinson, *A New Quest for the Historical Jesus* (Naperville, Ill.: A. R. Allenson, and London: S.C.M. Press, 1959), pp. 77, 94.

ble. What they do claim is that the kerygma has a historical context, namely, the person of Jesus, and is not adequately understood
when separated from it.

From this point of view one cannot say that historical research
legitimizes the kerygma in such a way as to dispense with the necessity for existential commitment; but one might say with Ebeling,
"If the quest of the historical Jesus were in fact to prove that faith
in Jesus has no basis in Jesus himself, then that would be the end
of Christology."[62] The discovery that faith in Jesus had no basis in
Jesus might not necessarily destroy the reality of God, but it would
at least alter our understanding of Him. In the words of Ronald
Hepburn, the engineer's, the painter's, and the native's view of a
particular landscape would be altered if the tree were cut down or
the river dammed up.[63] Surely there must be some connection between the Word of God and the words or events in which we
confront it. Otherwise, there would be no basis for its having a
meaning for us. To say this, however, is not to question or limit
divinity; it is to acknowledge the limits of humanity.

62. Ebeling, *Word and Faith*, p. 205.
63. Ronald Hepburn, *Christianity and Paradox* (London: Watts, 1958),
p. 108.

Faith and Truth

Faith for both Jaspers and Bultmann is in some sense a historical event. That is, faith is dependent upon the encounter with the transcendent from within the context of the historical tradition of man. In relation to the historical tradition man either awakens to the possibility of his Existenz (Jaspers) or he confronts the event of Jesus as the Christ as a repeatable possibility in his life (Bultmann). Thus they can speak of the truth of faith only in the context of man's historical being-in-the-world. Truth claims, which are either empirical in nature and abstracted from the subject or merely subjective in nature and abstracted from the object, have no relevance unless they are understood as part of the total situation of man's being-in-the-world.

From this perspective both Jaspers and Bultmann contrast the truth of faith and the truth of science and reason, which compares in some ways with the conclusions of the logical positivists, who, perhaps more than anyone else, are responsible for raising the question of truth in our time. It is well known that the earlier logical positivists equate meaning and empirical verification and consequently set aside religious and moral judgments as being of an emotive and hence non-cognitive nature. Yet, insofar as these thinkers have made clear the distinction between empirical and non-empirical judgments, their work has paralleled the work of the post-Kantian existentialist tradition to which both Jaspers and Bultmann belong. Jaspers and Bultmann also make a distinction between judgments requiring commitment or belief and judgments which may be considered universally valid. The truth of faith is not universally valid but is dependent upon the commitment of the believer, and thus in some sense the believer accepts responsibility for the truth of that which he proclaims.

Where Jaspers and Bultmann differ from the logical positivists, then, is not at the point of differentiating between the empirical and non-empirical but in refusing to limit the non-empirical to the realm of the emotive and non-cognitive. Neither Jaspers nor Bultmann ignores the disciplined inquiry that characterizes the realm of scientific investigation. In fact both might be understood to have contributed in some sense to this realm in their research in psychiatry and history. And both maintain the importance of this kind of inquiry into man's life in the world. What they do not say, however, is that veridical judgments are limited to the sphere of scientific investigation.

Jaspers and Bultmann are realists in the sense that their method is one which begins with life as it is lived, seeking to elucidate experience in its broadest context as opposed to limiting it in accordance with certain *a priori* assumptions. The result is not a denial of certain dimensions of experience but a description of their distinctive elements and references. Thus, empirical truth is understood as only one dimension of the total environment; truth is not something which stands apart from man's meaningful encounter with the world but follows from it. It follows that evidence applicable to any one dimension of experience is not final in relation to other dimensions and has its relevance for the other dimensions only insofar as it is understood in the total context of man's situation in the world.

If in this way, however, Jaspers and Bultmann may be understood to reply to the claims of positivists, they are still given no privilege which permits them to ignore the problem of verification or falsification in the larger context. That is, unless faith is to be restricted to the magic circle of the select few and unless it is to die the "death of a thousand qualifications," it must be able to present itself at least as a possibility which is meaningful in the context of reality as a whole. This Jaspers has sought to do in earnest. In relating philosophical faith to science, reason, and tradition he has sought to make clear the situation of a faith which transcends these criteria and yet would be nothing apart from them. Reason questioning its own presuppositions is shown to point toward fulfilment in faith, which never escapes the imperative to clarify itself in the context of the world. Thus, if Jaspers is not fully successful in clarifying the dimension of transcendent Being, he has at least not sought refuge from the complex problem of truth which faith continually confronts.

Bultmann, on the other hand, often seems to avoid a head-on confrontation with this problem and has with some right been criticized by Ronald Hepburn for insulating his claims against the claims of verification or falsification. Hepburn, in a spirit which reflects both his openness to inquiry and his striving for clarity, strikes at what he calls Bultmann's flight from the evidential. His criticism of Bultmann, which is similar to Anthony Flew's criticism of theology in general, is that Bultmann transforms any apparently hostile evidence, argument, or fact so that it yields positive support for a modified and freshly secured theological view.[64] Now it might be admitted that Hepburn's criticism that Bultmann ignores the contradictions within the New Testament by rising above them in the mythological, or that Bultmann rejects I Cor. 15:3–8 as evidence for the resurrection, can be explained in part through Hepburn's failure to grasp faith's claim that its object is not subject to empirical or *historisch* verification. But Hepburn's real point strikes home when he says that Bultmann in removing faith from the realm of the provable "has again omitted to argue for a vital proposition, namely that absence of evidence does not disqualify a religion from being acceptable by reasonable men, or that 'unprovable' here is not equivalent to 'baseless' or 'unfounded' as it undeniably is in many contexts."[65] In other words if Bultmann refuses to justify

---

64. Hepburn, "Demythologizing and the Problem of Validity," pp. 230 ff.
65. *Ibid.*, pp. 231–232.

faith in accordance with empirical or *historisch* data, then how will
he justify it, or will he admit simply that faith is without reason?

Bultmann maintains on several occasions that faith is not irra-
tional, and he certainly pictures faith as involving an understanding
of the self which is open to philosophical analysis. But he passes
over opportunities to answer directly the question of verification
or falsification. It is difficult, for instance, for one to reconcile his
saying that faith does not involve a *sacrificium intellectus* with his
saying that men must silence all voices before the Word of God.
Neither is it helpful when Bultmann dismisses Jaspers' question
concerning a criterion of revelation with: "As though God had to
justify himself to man!"[66] One can only gather that the reason
Bultmann finds no real conflict between reason and faith is that
they are somehow in different and unrelated dimensions of human
experience. Perhaps the closest that Bultmann comes to suggesting
a criterion of truth is in his Gifford Lectures where he proposes
that a *Weltanschauung* is most adequate which expresses adequately
the historicity of man.[67] But this is hardly more than a suggestion
and seen in the larger context of Bultmann's thought would seem
to have little relevance to the question of truth with regard to
speaking of an act of God.

It is perhaps Bultmann's silence on the subject of truth which is
most revealing. For while he has found it possible to present a
reasonable account of human existence through dependence upon
existential philosophy, he apparently denies philosophy its role as
critic of religious truth which speaks not only of human existence
but also of an act of God. Bultmann makes clear the distinction
between reason and faith, but he fails to show how they are also
related. Thus whatever his intention, faith often takes on the
appearance of an arbitrary decision made in the face of tradition
understood as law.

There is a sense, of course, in which religious or philosophical

66. *Myth*, p. 68; see also pp. 42, 80.
67. Bultmann, *History and Eschatology*, p. 149.

faith is self-authenticating. All reasoning originates from some belief. And we are at present no closer to a proof of our belief in the external world than we are to a *proof* of transcendent Being. But this does not relieve us of the responsibility of arguing for the reasonableness of our belief regarding reality. The problem is not really that of belief arguing against unbelief but of two or more beliefs about the world arguing for the reasonableness of their accounts. The problem is particularly acute with regard to belief in the world as rooted in the transcendent, for the object of faith is not definable in the ordinary sense of the word. Both Jaspers and Bultmann admit that the object of faith cannot be proven. But whereas Bultmann tends to speak as if we must choose between faith and reason, Jaspers argues that the relation between faith and reason must be made explicit. To ignore this interrelationship, it would seem, is to present a stumbling block to man which prevents him from arriving at the real stumbling block of the Christian faith.

At this point Bultmann would do well to listen to Jaspers. Jaspers maintains that he intended in his work, *Philosophie*, to make "a systematic study of the act of transcending: in philosophical world-orientation in order to loosen any possible enchainment to known things in the world; in the clarification of Existenz in order to recall and awaken to what man himself really is; in metaphysics in order to experience final limits and give intimations of Transcendence."[68] This statement of purpose is most suggestive with regard to the role of reason in faith. Reason cannot finally verify faith, but in the act of clarification it may indicate the limits of finite systems of the self and world and thus make possible an openness to the dimension in which faith has its being. Reason in this sense would not function as a proof but as an argument seeking to comprehend existence in empirical or rational terms and in failing to do this might open us up to the dimension in which transcendent Being discloses itself to existence.

68. *Reason*, p. 155, n. 4.

In this way Jaspers' philosophy might be said to indicate what Ian Crombie has called the reference range of theological statements.[69] The difficulty is that Jaspers has thus far done little more than this. Except for the relative experience of the individual, transcendent Being remains the unknown beyond the limit. Even when Jaspers turns to "revelation," it is to an inner awakening which is at best indefinite and obscure. Thus even if we are led to see that transcendent Being refers to that which is beyond ordinary thinking, we still fail to grasp more than the reference to a limit beyond which man cannot think. However, if one were able to supplement Jaspers' analysis with a more adequate ontology, it might supply a reasonable basis in relation to which religious faith could converse with man's understanding of himself in the world. Apart from this, God appears to be totally removed from the reality of the world, in which case faith appears to differ little from atheism, which denies that God has any reality in the world.

69. I. M. Crombie, "The Possibility of Theological Statements" in *Faith and Logic*, ed. Basil Mitchell (Boston: Beacon Press, and London: E. G. Allen, 1957).

V Summary and Conclusion

The aim of this study has been to make a contribution toward an understanding of some of the issues raised in the dialogue between Jaspers and Bultmann. In the course of this investigation a remarkable similarity between the thought of Jaspers and Bultmann regarding man's understanding of himself in the world has been revealed. Both point beyond the limits of a positivism that would restrict man's understanding of himself to the empirically verifiable. Both reject the building of rational systems as the way to truth. And both disclose the sense of risk and commitment that is basic to man's coming to an understanding of himself in relation to transcendent Being. Yet in the final analysis we are made aware of a significant boundary which separates philosophical faith and Christian faith and consequently philosophy and theology.

Philosophical faith challenges all attempts to think Being or God in concepts whose content is finished and complete. It is essentially faith in the inquiry of reason which, in foundering at the limits of understanding, intimates transcendent Being as the source of authentic selfhood. It is an interpretation of Being which paradoxically demands unconditional openness on the part of the believer. Bultmann presents Christian faith similarly insofar as he also understands that the object of faith cannot be restricted to concepts or doctrines. However, unlike Jaspers, Bultmann speaks as a theologian in the service of the community of faith. He speaks of an actual occurrence of the Word of God in the proclamation of the Church. Thus faith for Bultmann suggests something other than unconditional openness. Faith is a definite commitment on the part of the believer to the event of the Word which he has heard, and theology speaks out of this commitment.

This distinction stands always in the background of the discussion between Jaspers and Bultmann, and the failure to acknowledge it is at times responsible for their failure to communicate with each other in a genuine sense. Jaspers rightly demands that the theologian be open to the philosopher's critique of religious judgments and propositions. And surely he has some basis for saying that theologians often "fall silent, state an incomprehensible proposition, speak of something else, make some categoric statement, engage in amiable talk, without really taking cognizance of what one has said. . . ."[1] Even Bultmann seems to be guilty of this on occasions. But the theologian has the right to expect in return that the philosopher be open to the distinctive claim of the theologian to speak from within the "circle of faith." The theologian does not rest content with the questionableness of existence or the ambiguity of Being. He is responsible to the community, which believes that it hears a concrete Word addressed to faith in the proclamation of the Church. Jaspers seems at times unwilling to grant this distinctive role to theology and for this reason perhaps misses a part of what Bultmann is seeking to communicate.

A dialogue between philosophy and theology does not require that one abandon itself in favor of the other. But it does require that each be open to the particular task of the other. The theologian claims that God addresses man in this world. But if this is so the theologian cannot appear to use the results of the philosopher's inquiry only where it is convenient. He must also struggle in a genuine manner with the philosopher's critique of his judgments and propositions. Faith may in a sense transcend the rational analysis of the world but it cannot ignore it or contradict it without failing to communicate with man who lives in this world. On the other hand, the philosopher who concerns himself with religious ideas cannot claim to fulfil his task of analysis until he is open to

1. *Perennial Scope*, p. 77.

the peculiar task of theology to speak of an actual Word in the proclamation of the Church. The dialogue between the philosopher and the theologian is most fruitful when the theologian acknowledges the openness of communication in philosophy and the philosopher the commitment of faith on the part of the theologian.

Index of Names